Jamie Remembers

Growing Up in Eustis

Jim Greenlee

authorHOUSE®

AuthorHouse™
1663 Liberty Drive
Bloomington, IN 47403
www.authorhouse.com
Phone: 1 (800) 839-8640

Published by AuthorHouse 04/13/2015

ISBN: 978-1-5049-0537-4 (sc)
ISBN: 978-1-5049-0536-7 (e)

Library of Congress Control Number: 2015905257

Print information available on the last page.

DEDICATIONS

To my wife Sylvia Wing Greenlee for her encouragement and assistance.
To my parents, Herbert and Kathleen Greenlee, for their faithful
parenting.
To those wonderful people of Eustis, Florida, who in my childhood
assisted in my growing up process.
To my God Who has made my wonderful life what it is.

Contents

Prologue

Jamie Remembers takes a look at early life through the eyes of a child born into a happy family making our home in the central Florida town of Eustis. Though we were not greatly gifted materially during my childhood, we children were privileged to belong to parents who taught us of God's love for us and His providential care for our needs.

The idea for this series of vignettes from my early life was born in December of 2005, when while in my hometown of Eustis, Florida, I stopped by the office of the **EUSTIS NEWS** and subscribed to it. Upon receiving my first issue at my current home in Durham, North Carolina, I contacted the paper to see if it would like an article or two from someone who grew up in that town in the 1940s and 1950s. The paper indicated that it would. Shortly after I sent my first article, I was asked to write a column for the paper on a regular basis. I agreed to do this, and began to submit them in no particular chronological order, and all from the first 17 years of my life in Eustis.

These articles appeared regularly, not only in the **EUSTIS NEWS**, but also later in both the **TRIANGLE NEWS** and the **EUSTIS REFLECTIONS**, the Eustis Historical Society, Inc., newsletter.

I wish to thank each and every one of those whose names appear in my various articles. And also those who are not named herein, but who contributed greatly to many of these experiences of my early life.

I hope that my sharing of these childhood and teenage happenings will encourage others to record their growing up experiences, for it helps us to understand our family and community histories better. And it will be a valuable tool in helping future generations know and understand those who came before them. It has been my pleasure to write the **Growing Up in Eustis** articles.

Jim

1

In the Beginning

I drew my first breath and saw mama and others in the delivery room of Bartow General Hospital in Bartow, Florida at 7:30 a.m. on October 17th, 1937. Dr. Murphy, our family doctor, had just delivered the umpteenth baby of his long career. My folks and brother John were living in Eustis at the time, but mama gave birth to all of her children back in Bartow, her hometown.

When my parents, Herbert John Greenlee and Kathleen Demerest Anderson Greenlee, arrived in Eustis after marrying at my grandparents' home in Bartow in 1934, they rented a room from a Mrs. Mann on Orange Avenue. After John was born in 1936, they moved to a house on Morin Street near the Atwater Avenue intersection and also near the Eustis Airport.

But then my pending arrival necessitated an even larger house, and the move to Belmont Heights on the Old Mount Dora Road was in mid-1937. Our family was completed when sister Miriam came along in 1939.

So, my earliest recollections are from the early 1940s when we lived in Belmont Heights. Our house was located behind four large oak trees, which stood in a row across the front of the yard, and that still stand as of the date of this writing, in 2014. (The house was long ago moved to a spot near Trout Run, just north of the town of Eustis). Behind us and down the hill was beautiful West Crooked Lake.

John started to school in 1942, I followed a year later, and then Miriam joined us in 1945. During my first year of school, we rode a school bus, driven by Mrs. Gnann, from Belmont Heights to Eustis Elementary School on Citrus Avenue and Prescott Street. Mrs. Gnann was a friendly person who seemed almost an extension of everybody's family. She was good for little boys and girls just leaving mama for the first time to enter the world of academia. Pearl Ashford taught each of us in the first grade.

Those happy days for our family included long walks with daddy on Saturdays, usually on what is now called Eudora Road. In those days it was a clay road. Daddy, who was a great storyteller, would sit John, Miriam and me down on some stumps along that road and fill our ears with Bible stories as well as stories from his imagination.

We had a radio that worked intermittently. It was absent an outside case and we could see all the large tubes lighted up. That radio brought us much enjoyment as we listened to our favorite children's program, *Lets' Pretend*, and Daddy tuned it to the country music station, WCKY in Cincinnati, Ohio.

2

Remembering Just Like It Was Yesterday

Here's a little journey down memory lane from my family's days in Belmont Heights. I'm thinking John and I were 6 and 5 and the Christmas was probably in 1942. The folks had gotten pedal cars for us boys. And early Christmas morning we were absolutely thrilled at what Santa Claus had left us under the tree! John's pedal car was a fire truck and mine was a roadster. Don't rightly remember what Miriam got that year, but we boys considered that a totally satisfactory Christmas! In those days the four oak trees across the front yard were smaller and we could drive those pedal cars between them. Those cars furnished us joy for several years.

Early in the mornings we would watch and listen for the "Troo-Loo." The Troo-Loo was actually a truck hauling workers that would come around the "S" curve near the house. I suppose it never occurred to the driver to back shift as he slowed down to make the curve. The truck would be going at a walking pace by the time it straightened out coming toward our house. And the engine labored to pick up speed again while in high gear. It sounded like *troo....loo....loo....loo....loo* to us, hence it's nickname. Watching for and waving at the folks in the Troo-Loo was a part of our childhood routine.

A favorite play toy for me was a Phillips Milk of Magnesia blue bottle. Now, that's the nastiest medicine Mama ever foisted off on us kids, but I thought the bottle was neat. In those days there was both the Greyhound Bus Line and the Florida Motor Lines that came to Eustis. I fancied myself as the driver of a Florida Motor Lines bus and the Magnesia bottle was the bus. One side of our front yard was mostly dirt and I had little roads on quite an area of it. I picked up and dropped off hundreds of passengers at the various stops. I remember that my greatest desire was to be a Florida Motor Lines bus driver when I grew up. But by the time I had come of age that bus line was defunct, the blue bottle had been tossed and I had become interested in other careers.

3

Mr. Merck, our Hero

In those early 1940 days, there was quite a distance between our house on the Old Mount Dora Road in Belmont Heights and West Crooked Lake down the hill behind us, probably a hundred yards or so. This expanse was mostly weeds and little scrubby trees. It was a great place to hunt gophers and roam around for two little boys and their small sister.

Now, in those days quite a few of the houses in country settings likes ours had "trash piles" out back where you would simply burn your trash. Our trash pile was in a location that the folks considered safely removed from both the house and that field behind us. But one day an incident concerning that burning trash pile caused us children, and Mom when she found out, some scary moments!

We kids were playing perhaps a little too close to the flames. I am not sure of the details of what started it, but the fire suddenly spread from that burning heap to the dry and ready-to-burn weeds of that field! Terrified, we boys tried briefly to put it out but it grew rapidly in size! In no time, a rather good-sized blaze was burning its way down the hill.

After quick assessment of the situation, Mom scurried across the road to the Merck house. I reckon the Lord knew the one Mom should turn to for help! Because we watched a man, one that we considered our hero afterward, go into action.

Of all things, while we watched in horror, Mr. Merck began to set a series of fires farther down the hill, below the oncoming fire! What was he doing? Well, as his little fires began to spread, he easily put them out on the downhill side, leaving the fires on the up side to burn toward the oncoming large fire!

We learned that day what a "back fire" is! In just a few minutes the big fire was subdued when the fires met. What could have been a serious fire due to other houses being located nearby was extinguished with no further incident!

I am sure that future times of play near the burning trash pile were undertaken with greater caution!

I'll be back firing another episode at you again soon!

4

Sawdust Pile Fun until...

This time I share memories of sawdust piles. That's right. In the early days in Belmont Heights, Daddy would take us for walks on Saturdays. (We were blessed to have a dad whose choice of worship day freed him from work during the daylight hours on Saturdays.) It was just a short walk to the corner of Old Mount Dora Road and Eudora Road.

Sometime before we moved to Belmont Heights, there had been a saw mill at that corner. The mill was long gone as was the visible sawdust pile that accompanied it. But we children learned from daddy that fires can burn below the surface of the ground for a very long time. Evidently at some point the sawdust pile had caught fire and had been extinguished and perhaps the remainder that had not burnt had been moved away. But not all of it.

Although the location looked as if there had never been a sawdust pile there, we could dig just under the surface in that spot and often find live sparks! Even as a child I marveled at the ability of those sparks to remain alive though buried.

Further down Eudora Road was an active sawmill on the right side of the road. There was a very large sawdust pile there. Daddy would take us to that one, and we would romp and play until our clothes were full of sawdust! We found that we could jump from pretty high up and find a cushioned landing! Our visits to that sawdust pile took place even after we moved to Barnes Avenue. And some of our circle of friends from our new neighborhood would sometimes go with us.

The only accident that I remember taking place among us in connection with that sawdust pile happened to Miriam, my sister. It was my fault to be truthful. She was on top of the pile and I shoved her off of it. Upon landing, she encountered a sharp sliver of wood that stood upright just under the surface. That one brought an abrupt ending to our fun that day, a justified guilt trip for me, and Miriam carrying a few stitches for awhile.

Ah, but she survived, I got over the guilt, and we remained close afterwards. So I close this episode with a reminder for all kids to inspect the landing area before you shove any of your friends or family members off the local sawdust pile! And try to shake most of that sawdust from your clothes before putting them in the laundry basket. Mom'll love you for it.

5

Ahhh...Blueberries (Not)

This memory takes place around 1941 or 42 out on West Crooked Lake where I lived in my early life, in Belmont Heights. Daddy's grandfather from Indiana had come to live with us. Though walking with a cane at that time, he was still "spry" enough to get around quite nicely and even to take walks with us kids sometimes. This one has to do with one of these walks.

John, Miriam and I were walking with Grandpa one Saturday after he came home from church. We had walked to the "S" curve on the Old Mt. Dora Road, located about 300 yards from our house. And what a treasure we found there! Growing wild all over the place were blueberries! Luscious blueberries! Grandpa took a look at them and said it was okay to eat them. And eat them we did!

After awhile we returned home, blue stains all around our mouths and on our hands. Immediately our concerned mother asked where these stains came from! We told her of the great time we had had in eating those blueberries down at the curve. Whoa! Mama knew that there were no blueberries growing wild around there anywhere!

So we marched with her down to the corner to show her our "find." Folks, to her further consternation, she found that we had all three ingested what she knew as "Deadly Nightshade!" I'm not sure what the real name of it is, but a terrified mother hustled us home and went across to the neighbor's to call Dr. Louis Bowen, our family doctor.

He advised her to "doctor" us with a healthy dose of Milk of Magnesia (the antidote for many an ailment in my childhood). And to watch us for any hint of an adverse reaction to the berries. As I recall, we each one made it through this crisis with no ill effects. And Grandpa got a quick lesson on not allowing us to eat anything on our walks without her knowledge and approval.

Blueberries are still my favorite berry even after that, folks!

6

Young Service Station Attendants

I remember the excitement in our family the day that Daddy drove up in a 1929 Model A Ford! It was an old car by then, but seemed like a new one to us! He had swapped his Model T Ford that had just about seen it's day. This was in the days of gasoline rationing because of the war, and the windshield of the Model A sported two decals, an A and a B, that indicated he used his car for getting to work as well as for other activities.

That car was our family transportation for a number of years in the early 1940s, both in Belmont Heights and at Barnes Avenue. It had a storied history in our family and deserves a hallowed place in my memories.

There was a time though, that sister Miriam and I almost did that poor car in! Children today do not know what a "full service" filling station is. Most of us pump our own gasoline, pay with a card at the pump, and are gone. Not so in those days! We were used to having an attendant come out, ask how many gallons we wanted and so forth. (A dollar would get you between 4 and 5 gallons back then!) And that gentleman would also check your oil and radiator levels, and wash your windshield. That was standard operating procedure.

I reckon Miriam was 4 years old or so and I a year older. And we decided to "service" daddy's car! Now the 1929 Ford had both the gasoline tank and radiator caps at either end of the hood. And it was time to fuel that vehicle!

Having seen the car fueled by a station attendant before, we knew which cap covered the gasoline tank. So we crawled up there and removed the cap closest to the windshield. Then Miriam got down and took an empty

Animal Cracker box and filled it to the brim with good ole Greenlee front yard dirt! That's right, folks!

Carefully she climbed back up there and emptied the contents of that box right into the tank! This she did a couple of times! And then the cap was securely replaced. We had a very unhappy father as he was told of the type of "service" we had done on his car for him!

There was a saving mechanism in that tank that Ford had thoughtfully installed, thank goodness! A strainer was located a few inches down the pipe to the tank. Daddy dipped out all the dirt that he could, and that device caught most of the rest of it! He then carefully removed it, and for the remainder of the car's life with our family the tank had no strainer.

Early on after this incident, the car's engine would occasionally buck and kick as a few of the dirt particles worked their way through it. But it never quit! And I guarantee that we never played "gas station" again with that car!

Don't "fuel" around with your folk's cars, kids!

7

A Good Drink of West Crooked Lake

I reckon that this was as near me drowning as I have ever gotten so far! I must have been five or maybe just turned six. It was before we moved from Belmont Heights out the Old Mount Dora Road to Barnes Avenue in Eustis, and that move took place in late 1943.

Our house was located up the hill from West Crooked Lake. A two-rut road to the lake ran down between our house and that of the Arnold's. A cleared area on the shore and in the lake made it a nice place to swim. This day would be like many others, with the little Greenlee family walking down to the swimming hole. Only it wasn't "a usual day" for me! Or for the rest of my family for that matter!

Mama, as she always did, stayed in the very shallow water where Miriam and usually I would cavort around in safety. John, being a little older, would venture out a little deeper with Daddy keeping a weather eye on him. Sometimes Mama and Daddy would trade off for a few minutes, so she could swim.

I must have decided on my own that day that it was time for me to venture out into the deeper water! Now I could not swim a lick at that time (which is only slightly less than I can do now). But the sand under my feet did not indicate a steep slope and I felt quite safe in my exploratory venture.

Mama seemed not to notice my movement toward trouble, nor did Daddy or John. But, hey, things were fine as the water reached shoulder level.

Maybe just a little father out, I thought. But as the water reached the top of my neck, the pressure of it began to push me deeper! I had not planned on this. I got light on my feet and any effort in walking towards the safety of the shallows resulted in my going backwards, even deeper!

Suddenly the water was at mouth level! I'm not sure why I didn't holler before, but now I could not even yell for help without getting a mouthful! I began thrashing around, coughing and choking, and boy did I get the attention then! Daddy made a lunge for me and hustled me to the beach! I remember being quite strangled as he did some sort of artificial respiration on me!

Mama told me this more than I remember it, but when I was finally able to gasp out a few words, I said "This is the end of my life!" Well, that statement proved to be wrong, as in just a few minutes I was up and dabbling a little in the very shallow water again.

But if Daddy had not been there at the moment, very probably I would not be writing this episode now!

Keep your water wings or a parent handy, kids!

8

The "Jamie-John"

Delving very deeply into my Belmont Heights memories I recall a swing that Daddy made for John and me in 1940 or 41. Well, I reckon Miriam had a turn in it sometimes, too. But it was fashioned to look like an airplane with two seats in it. On the sides were the words, *The Jamie-John*. Some things about it I probably remember more by being told about it, as John and I were 5 and 4 when we "flew that thing."

It had a propeller that could be turned from inside by the one of us in the front seat. I am told that I continually referred to the prop as a "muh-pella". My parents once overheard brother John bring me some educational advice. He said, "Jamie, it's not a "muh-pella"; it's a "buh-pella." (To think that I would go on to join the Air Force where I would be surrounded by huge *Jamie-John's* with lots of "buh-pella's" on them! Sure happy I did not refer to them as "muh-pella's!" Thanks, Brother!)

This fun machine hung from one of the four oak trees closely lining the front of our yard in Belmont Heights. Don't rightly remember what happened to it.

Another great toy Daddy made for us was a quite large bomber with engines on each wing. We could pick it up and with John holding one wing and me the other, we could fight the World War II enemies of America as we raced through the yard.

Due to the economics of our little family in those times, we kids didn't have many store-bought toys and playthings. But we had a dad that kept us furnished with great stuff like the aforementioned that he fashioned with his own hands. Our lives were very full in those early childhood times.

9

Early Appliances in Our Home

I mentioned in a previous article that our home entertainment center when we lived in Belmont Heights in the early 1940s was a radio that did not have a case on it. And I remembered the glowing tubes as we listened to it. And our cook stove was fueled by kerosene. To light it, you would turn the flow of kerosene on, lift up the side of a burner and light the wick that circled below it. Then to spread the flame, you would take the handle and shake it back and forth. That helped it ignite the entire circle. The heat could be regulated with a little knob that would raise or lower the wick.

We had an ice box instead of an electric refrigerator which was not unusual in those days. It was round with a lid on top that covered the compartment holding a block of ice. I'm not sure how often the ice had to be replenished, but I know it was on a regular basis.

The ice man would park his truck, come around to the back of it and open the door. Then he would take an ice pick and chip off a block of ice that would fit our ice box. This he would pick up with his ice tongs and bring it to the kitchen. It was great fun to have the ice man visit. Because we kids could have all of the little ice chips lying around after he was finished at the truck.

When we moved to Barnes Avenue in 1943, for a time we again had a kerosene cook stove, but after several years the folks bought a small propane gas kitchen stove. Also the ice box was replaced by a small Crosley Shelvadore refrigerator. These two appliances were used through the years until Dad died in 1987 and Mom moved to North Carolina to live with my family.

Our heat in both Eustis locations was a wood-burning heater until we children were quite large. Then Dad replaced it with one that was fueled by kerosene. On Barnes Avenue it was in a central location in our home; actually in the dining room. It did pretty well at heating the rather small house.

One nicety we did without in our growing up years was a water heater. We always heated our bath water in a kettle on the kitchen stove, and toted it in to the tub. Brother John and I took care of that situation when as grownups we had a water heater installed for the folks.

I know that some of the things I mention in this article have never been experienced by some, especially those in the current generation. Thank God for the things that most of us now take for granted, but that were hard to come by for some of us in generations past.

10

"Buckshot" and the Chicken

In the early 1940s days in Belmont Heights, Buckshot and his family lived next to us, just across the little two-rut dirt road that went down to West Crooked Lake behind us. Don't know why everybody called him "Buckshot", but the following little incident might give us a clue.

I reckon Buckshot and his family were planning to have chicken for dinner, but he was having a very hard time catching the chicken that had other plans for her future. John and I were in the yard watching the chicken chase take place. And racing around Buckshot's house and under it, that chicken made it interesting! Finally Buckshot had had enough!

Going into his house, he soon returned with a shotgun! A shotgun? John and I were not used to being around firearms of any kind! So we watched with rapt attention as Buckshot stationed himself at the side of the house near the back. His son was rounding the front of the house, chasing the chicken.

With shotgun to his shoulder, Buckshot shouted, "Where is he, son?" "There he is! There he is!" came the shouted reply! And at that moment the hapless chicken came barreling around the corner of the house and into the sights of Buckshot's gun!

BLAM! Feathers flew as the chicken's fate was sealed! That was the first time we boys had ever seen anything of this sort! We replayed that scene in our own yard games many times.

11

Adventures of "Johnny Oat"

Ahhh... breakfast time in the Greenlee household of the early 1940s. Seems like a staple for young John, Jamie and Miriam was oatmeal! Never mind that it was both cheap and good for us; we just didn't care for it! I know we had a frustrated Mama because of it.

Now enter Daddy. He had a very fertile mind and could entertain us for a long time by story-telling. Often his stories were episodes from the Bible, but to assist Mama in getting the oatmeal down us, he invented a new character: Johnny Oat!

I remember sitting there with my bowl brimming with oatmeal awaiting the latest episode in Johnny's life. Daddy would begin to spin the new adventure. He would tell the story and every 3 or 4 sentences he would pause and say, "Take a bite!". Three little spoons would rise to 3 little mouths in obedience.

Don't know how Daddy managed to come up with so many new involvements in the life of Johnny Oat, but his adventures sure helped the Greenlee children of Belmont Heights get down a lot of oatmeal!

MIRIAM, JOHN & JAMIE

12

Our Neighbor, the War Casualty

An incident I remember from the World War II days took place in probably 1942, when the surprise attack at Pearl Harbor had taken place only months before. I don't remember the actual event of Pearl Harbor (I was four). But a man, accompanied by his wife and carrying a shotgun, came to our front porch in Belmont Heights, and he pleaded with Mama to get us kids and accompany his wife and him as they were walking out of harm's way. He warned Mama that the orange grove across from our house on the Old Mount Dora Road was just full of enemy soldiers!

Mama thanked him for the warning and promised to keep us safe in the house. With a knowing nod to Mama, the woman encouraged her husband to continue on toward Eudora Road. The poor gentleman was evidently a casualty of the war without ever firing a shot in it.

I recall the "scrap drives" during the war. Each family was to save all scrap metal and it would be picked up occasionally for the war effort. I understood that it would be melted down and re-used for military equipment. The scrap drives may have included more than just metal.

Though I was too young to fully appreciate what the citizenry did in the war effort in the 1940s, I have seen the American people pull together as one in current times of national emergency. We are a blessed and wonderful people!

13

Hello Barnes Avenue

In late 1943 we moved from Belmont Heights to Barnes Avenue in Eustis, and the remainder of my childhood and through my middle teen years were spent there

 When we arrived, ours was the only house on our side of the road on Barnes Avenue in the block between Grove and Center Streets. It had a garage out back and sported a small cellar, too. The folks paid $3,000 for the property. Barnes Avenue was a clay road in those days and traffic was very light. That made it a great extension of our yard as we played various games of ball on it during the day and "kick the can" during the evenings.

Not too long after we settled in at our new place, we got a telephone. Our first one. It sat proudly on top of our Philco console radio. It had a big silver button that would pop up when you picked up the receiver. A pleasant voice would then inquire: "Number please?" (My Aunt Rachel was one of those pleasant voices.) Numbers in Eustis consisted of 3 numbers and a color. Ours was 3-2-1 Green. What a great invention! It was quite a novelty in the Greenlee household.

After several years, we got our first neighbor on our side of the road. No more roaming that empty lot, setting my gopher traps. (That was okay. I never caught one anyhow.) The Driggers soon lived next door, and were fine neighbors. They and the Hammond family and Mrs. Haines, both living on the other side of Barnes Avenue, comprised the population of our little road in 1945 or so.

Our neighborhood furnished John, Miriam and me with a number of great playmates in the 40s and early 50s, and they often gathered at our house. I will name some of these friends of that day, realizing that I will unintentionally omit a few. They were Tommy, Donny, Sally and Betty Lu Tippins, Jerry Lloyd Davis, Raymond Parrish, Dale and Janet Bartholomew, Barbara Branch, Harold Webb, Lewis Holland, Alton Crawford, David Ayers, James Mackessey, Jim McWhorter, Jean  Sawyer, and Earla Sue and Dallas Thompson.

It was along about 1944 that Daddy moved his shoe shop from Eustis Street to the inside of the Post Office arcade. His shop would no longer be in the lineup of stores in that block between Magnolia and Orange Avenues, stores that included Brown's Hardware, Bennett's Grocery, Brady's Dress Shop, Dollar's Fish Market, Strong's Sporting Goods, The Eustis Telephone Exchange and Coursey's Dry Cleaners among others. But Daddy's hand-painted sign hung over the Orange Avenue entrance. It read **Greenlee's Shoe Shop**, and the smaller letters beneath it boasted, *"Five Generations of Shoe Repair"*. (Shoe repair in my branch of the Greenlee family did not make it into the 6th generation.)

GREENLEE'S
SHOE SHOP FLOAT
WBP 1940+

The Post Office arcade had two entrances, one from Eustis Street and the other from Orange Avenue. Probably to the chagrin of postal employees and customers alike, we children found the arcade a great place to play. We did things like flying huge newspaper airplanes over customer's heads and even riding our bikes in there. (Okay, I know we shouldn't have...)

The country was still at war, and I remember the display of a miniature submarine that had been captured from our enemy. It sat on a wooden stand downtown for a short period of time. I got claustrophobic just looking at it.

Well, gotta go. I'll be back.

14

Remembering the Eustis Schools

The war in Europe was over! To us children of early elementary school age in 1945 it probably was not a particularly exciting occurrence unless we had a relative directly involved in it. All we had known in our short lives since we were old enough to remember was the war in Europe and in the Pacific.

But Eustis Elementary School realized the importance of the proceedings on that May 8th day. The principal came to every room and had each class stand or sit along the walls of the hall. Somewhere far down that hall there was a radio blaring the good news for all of us to hear. I remember the teacher telling us that though we might not fully understand what was going on, this was a very important historical event. I was a second grader at this time in Jenny Newell's class.

In the middle and late 1940s, Mama (Kathleen) was a substitute teacher at the elementary school. So it was comforting for me (and a little embarrassing sometimes) to have Mama that close for extended periods. I admit to being a classic "mama's boy". Mr. Slaton was the principal during those years and his daughter Linda was in my class. Belle Byrd was in charge of the lunchroom downstairs.

The elementary school had classes through the 6th grade. From there our junior high years included the 7th and 8th grades, and we were housed with the senior high classes of 9th through the 12th grades in the same building, the Eustis High School on Washington Avenue. The High School in those days was an imposing white building, but I see that at some point during the intervening years it has had a beautiful expansion and facelift.

Jim Greenlee

Principals of the high school that I recall are Mr. Godbold, Mr. Wilson, and Chester Crowder, whom I remember quite well. I was familiar with the inside of his office. Mr. Crowder was faithful in helping me solve my disciplinary problems through those years. (We'll leave that one right there.) Head football coaches that I remember are Coach Hershey and Coach Charlie Broadway. And also Coach Bill Kelsey who coached our baseball team.

In 1955, my class graduated 34, and was one of the smallest of EHS classes ever. We all went our separate ways, some to college, some to the service, and some to who knows where. A few did remain in Eustis and close by and still do to this day. We had our 50th class reunion last year and it was good to see many of them again! And it is great to know that in our own ways we have contributed to society, and are still doing so. I want you to know, dear reader, that the credit goes in large part to the wonderful teachers in the Eustis school system of the 1940s and 1950s.

15

Washington's Birthday Adventures

In my childhood, Washington's Birthday was a big deal! It was celebrated in Eustis by a parade and a carnival. The parade began near the corner of Center Street and Magnolia Avenue, near Dr. Bowen's office. I remember that as being near the spot because for some years I participated in it in various capacities. The parade would come straight down Magnolia and end in Ferran Park.

One time I was dressed up like Uncle Sam and walked ahead of the parade. That was pretty gutsy for this shy boy, but I kinda liked it. I must have been in the 3rd or 4th grade. For another parade, Daddy, who was very handy at doing innovative things, advertised his shoe shop in an unusual way. He took poster board and fashioned a very large hatchet and an equally big hammer like he used in his shop. Brother John got inside the hammer and I was in the hatchet. We peered out holes cut for our faces and the handles came down to our knees. We walked side by side in the parade with lettering on both sides of the large paper tools. On the hatchet they read: "George used this" and on the hammer, "Greenlee uses this". Daddy also designed and built several floats, winning the prize one year.

My final appearance in the February 22nd, 1955 parade was a bit of an embarrassment for me. I was in the EHS Band, but had only been in it for a short time. Marching was not my strong suit! Well, here we were on Magnolia Avenue in the middle of town, near the Eustis Street crossing, when the whole parade stopped. Mr. Douthit, the bandmaster, took that occasion to have the band do a maneuver where it turns in on itself and ends up going the other way. I got lost immediately! So there I was, waving a big sousaphone (we called it a tuba back then) and running along beside the band until I finally spied my assigned spot, kindly left vacant by those near it. Mama and Daddy thought I did great!

EHS BAND
WASHINGTON'S BIRTHDAY PARADE

A carnival was always set up in Ferran Park for the occasion. There would be some rides and booths where we could spend the few coins we might have. All in all, it was great fun and we looked forward to Washington's Birthday each year.

But Miriam and I were a bit jealous of our brother John, because he had the audacity to be born on February 22nd! So for his birthday every year, school would be out and we would have this great big celebration! He never once went to school on his birthday! Tch!

16

Lake Gracie, My Favorite Swimming Hole

Before the building of the new Eustis swimming pool behind the McClelland Band Shell in Ferran Park, and even afterwards, there were favorite swimming holes around. Lake Joanna was a great place to swim, especially for a novice like this little guy. The water was shallow for quite a distance from shore, and many a happy time was had out there.

But my favorite was the little public swimming hole on Lake Gracie. Much of the time it was crowded with people both in and out of the water. The town had put in a metal "L"-shaped dock and the water was deep enough to dive off of it at the far end. Since it was located right down the hill from Eustis High, we fellas, while walking home from school, would sometimes stop and take a dip. Not having a bathing suit with us posed no problem. Now folks, we did not skinny-dip! (We wouldn'a done that…heh…heh.) We just stripped down to our dungarees and plunged in. They would be mostly dry by the time we got home.

Many of us took swimming lessons there. I remember helping several little guys who should have taken swimming lessons, back to shallow water. And also there was the time that I, while seeking to impress a girl or two who most probably were not looking anyhow, tried to dive backwards. I misjudged the distance I was from the edge and landed on the small of my back on the unforgiving metal edge of the dock. A "Greg Louganis" (of Olympic diving fame) I was not. But a little time on the beach and I was right back in.

One day while diving I noticed a shiny object on the bottom. I scooped up a beautiful ring! My folks tried to locate the owner through the Eustis News, but nobody claimed it. I still wear it as I write this article decades later. A friend asked me to find him a ring, too. So he and I dug into the sand in the shallow water, and darned if I didn't come up with another ring – a gold one with a diamond in the corner! It had initials on it, and the grateful owner was soon located. No telling the treasures that might still be the in the sand at that now defunct swimming hole!

Nothing tastes better than a bowl of cold dewberries with a little sugar sprinkled on them! Dewberries grew wild around the edge of Lake Gracie in those days. We as a family would go and pick to our fill while they were in season. I wonder if anybody kept some of those vines as that side of the road was developed.

I claim partial responsibility for any alligators found in Lake Gracie. Probably in 1951, my biology teacher, Vera Watkins, was dating the man she later married, Buck Dandridge. One day Buck brought two baby alligators to our class. Friend Bill Andrews was given one and I took the other. So there I was with an alligator but devoid of any knowledge of the care and feeding of my new pet! After keeping him penned up for a couple of weeks and trying to feed him stuff he wouldn't eat, I took him down to Lake Gracie and let him go. For the several years that I remained at Eustis High, I would walk past the lake and sometimes see a rather young alligator. I liked to think it was him.

I envied some of my friends of that day who lived close to Lake Gracie. Among others, there were Wayne (Gator) and Gail Thompson, Lee and Susan Sample, Phil Hill, Chubby Bartholomew, Ronnie and Raehn Davis, Edward and Emily Brown, Jerry Clark and Bill Andrews. Their locations to the swimming hole were wonderful!

17

Sandlot and Town Team Softball and Baseball

Town team softball! Now who could forget that? In the 1940s and 50s, various town businesses sponsored softball teams. Seems it had pretty much died out by the time I left for the Air Force in 1955. All of the games were played on several nights during the week, on the very nicely lighted softball field behind Eustis High School. We as a family would go as often as we could. It was great to sit on the wide concrete steps behind home plate, and watch people like Elzie Givins pitch!

Some of the teams were Jason's Groceteria, Brown's Hardware, Palm Pharmacy, Igou's Farm Store, Polk Buick and Shorty's Taxi. There were several others that escape my memory now. Each team had a snappy uniform shirt. Raymond Slaven was the very animated umpire, and sluggers like Ray Gatch, Tommy Branton and Jimmy Cincogranni made the games extremely interesting! My brother John, although younger than most of the players, did substitute on one of the teams because of his hitting skills. Folks, the entertainment was cheap and it was very good! Great softball was played there. A hat would be passed to help pay for the lights.

In those days Eustis also had a town baseball team, and we would play teams from Umatilla, Mount Dora, Apopka, Tavares and Leesburg as well as other towns. For a nominal fee, you could get a good evening's entertainment at the old Eustis Baseball Park out beyond the airport. Several names come to mind from our team back then: Lewis Marshall, again Ray Gatch and Tommy Branton, Perry Kirkland, and Harry Bailes. Harry had been a professional baseball player and was a real asset to the team. The games were well attended, and the parking lot was usually full. One night a Eustis player hit a long foul ball and it busted the windshield of his own truck!

The folks had bought the vacant lot next to us on Barnes Avenue. And we laid out our own softball diamond in that lot. Many a game was played there while a radio sitting in John's bedroom window blared the Major League Game of the Day, narrated by the Old Scotsman, Gordon McClendon. (It was years before we found out that he was not actually at the games, but was recreating the play by play from ticker tape.)

There was a catch to playing on that field, though. It wasn't really big enough for softball, and a well-hit ball to left field had to clear Barnes Avenue and go over the power wires to be a homerun. A not-so-well-hit ball to right field had to clear a row of arborvitae bushes that surrounded a little orange grove to be a homer.

Quite often the softballs ended up in neighbor's yards and sometimes hit their houses, including Mrs. Haines' tin roof. (These "tin roof" hits on her house would often bring her out shouting that she was going to call the "shh-reeef" on us!) "House hits" caused the field to empty while players ran to hide behind our house! In those cases, ball-retrieval was both daring and difficult. Despite this annoyance, my brother John managed to break Babe Ruth's homerun record of 60 in one summer season. We were proud of him, but folks, that's a lot of running, hiding, daring to retrieve and apologizing if confronted by the homeowner!

18

Fun with Daddy's Wire Recorder

Television came into its own during my childhood. I never dreamed of such until I saw my first one in the arcade window of Ayers Radio shop on Orange Avenue. I stood amazed with a group of people as we gawked at a moving picture coming from a large box! The signal came from station WMBR-TV in Jacksonville, which was one of only several cities in Florida with a television station. Though television was quite common by 1950, our family did not have a set until after I had left Eustis for the Air Force in 1955.

One luxury we did have, however, was a Webster-Chicago Wire Recorder that Daddy purchased in 1947. This gadget was a forerunner of the tape recorder, and was used by the military in the early and mid-1940s. The recordings were made on wire just a little larger in diameter than the human hair. We Greenlees had great sport with it! But I want to tell you what Daddy did with it once. The fire whistle would blow at noon every day. Located only a block away, that whistle really made a racket inside the Eustis Post Office arcade where Daddy's shoe shop was located. One day he recorded it at full volume on his wire recorder.

Important to this story is the fact that the Post Office had a big clock of some sort that they boasted was always right. And also, that the Post Office closed at noon on Wednesdays. Well, it being a Wednesday, Daddy set his little electric clock in his shop window to be about 3 minutes fast. He then went to the Post Office window and, in the course of conversation, told the postmaster (a Mr. Marley I think) that his big clock was 3 minutes slow. "It's never slow, Herb. It's always right with the noon whistle," came the reply. They finally agreed to see which clock was right by the noon whistle. (Do you see this one coming?)

When Daddy's clock showed 12:00 noon, he switched on his wire recorder at full volume! The arcade echoed as usual with the sound of that whistle! All the Post Office windows slammed shut as it closed for the afternoon! Three minutes later the arcade echoed again with the sound of the *real* whistle! Raised voices could be heard from within the Post Office! They were not at all amused by Daddy's prank!

After I had left Eustis, Daddy gave that wire recorder to David Ayers, my friend and son of Loy B. Ayers who owned the Radio shop. Several years ago David did me a great favor by giving it to me. Though it is presently inoperable, each time I see it, my mind goes back to those hours of fun we had with it all those years ago.

19

My Favorite Teen Hang-outs

Remember the Dreamboat restaurant? Don't know when it was torn down or taken away, but when I was a youngster it stood at the intersection of south Bay Street (I reckon it was actually Highway 19) and the road to Tavares. The Dreamboat was a real excursion boat that had been moved to that spot from Lake Eustis where it had spent many years of its aquatic life, and turned into a restaurant. I remember Mrs. Gnann stopping the school bus there and picking up kids in 1943.

Other places to eat come to mind. The Green Tile restaurant was on Bay Street at the intersection of Barnes Avenue, the street where we lived after moving into town. The neon sign on top of that green tile roof used to read "Frog Leg Shrimp Dinner". I remember thinking that was real strange. Surely nobody would eat frog legs! Yuk! Truly, I lived a sheltered life!

But probably the one that stands out over all the others was the Dixie Drive In. It was located between Eustis and Mount Dora at the intersection of Highway 19 and Highway 441, right about where Eudora Road cuts in. (I hope that I got the highway numbers correct.) The Dixie was the designated "hang out" for the teens of Eustis! I reckon it was for the Mount Dora kids, too, but I don't remember seeing many of them there.

Evenings and especially Friday and Saturday nights would find row upon row of cars parked in front of it, and on the inside it was standing room only! The jukebox was playing songs like "Moments to Remember" by the Four Lads, "He" by Al Hibbler and "Sincerely" by the McGuire Sisters. That tenderloin sandwich they made there still has to be the best sandwich I ever put in my mouth!

And the Dairy Freeze on Bay Street in Eustis was another popular spot. The parking lot was not as large as the Dixie's but we would crowd in there, too. Seems it began to become the new "hang out" for many of us in the mid-50s, I reckon for one reason because it was actually in Eustis. But the Dixie had to be my all-time favorite!

A favorite place for our family to get great food was King's Barbeque way out E. McDonald Avenue and up Palmetto Road. Mr. King sure knew how to do chicken! He would cook it with his own special sauce on it. He would take a breast, paint his sauce on it again, and wrap it in two slices of white bread and roll it up in waxed paper. Daddy would bring that stuff home and Lord have mercy, we would have a feast!

Shoot, folks, I've made myself hungry! So I'm goin' to the refrigerator for a while. Check in with you later.

20

Our Antics and Police Non-Amusement

Willis V. McCall was the Lake County sheriff through the years of my childhood. And the main players that I recall in Eustis law enforcement in the late 1940s and early 1950s were Jimmy Dickerson, Chief of Police, and Dick Shirk, his Deputy.

I recall a tragic event that occurred in Lake Dicie. A toddler wearing a cap pistol and holster had been standing up in a motorboat. The boat swerved and out he went! The weight of the pistol caused him to sink rapidly to the bottom of that very deep sinkhole lake. When we kids arrived on the scene (not far down Grove Street from where we lived), there was Dick Shirk diving time and again into that lake. The little lad was found later by other means, much too late to save his life. But we looked upon Dick Shirk as a hero.

Now, we boys in the neighborhood around Barnes Avenue were not bad kids. Mischievous a little… maybe… sometimes… but not really bad. There was this one incident I reckon I'll admit to: It started out harmless enough one evening. We found a rabbit that had been killed on Grove Street. One of the boys brought his rod and reel and we hooked the rabbit to it. After placing the rabbit on the other side of Grove Street we backed up Barnes Avenue probably a hundred feet. When we saw the lights of oncoming cars, a furious turning of the reel brought that rabbit carcass right out in front of them. There was some slamming on of brakes and horn blowing.

Well, rabbits like that only last so long. So we graduated to a length of garden hose, and when pulled it looked like a huge snake! More screeching and horn tooting! One dark night we guys were gathered on Barnes Avenue near our house, planning another night of fun, when around the corner of Grove and Barnes came the unmistakable police car of Dick Shirk. Terrified, most of us ran behind our house. We were soon rounded up, though, and sitting on our front steps with Policeman Shirk putting the fear of God into us.

Talking about being "scared straight!" We were told to report the next Saturday morning to the courtroom downstairs under the City Hall right next to the Public Library on the corner of Orange Avenue and Grove Street. You could have heard a pin drop in that place as a group of wide-eyed young teens listened carefully to a lecture given by Police Chief Jimmy Dickerson. That was the end of our season of mischief (of this type anyhow).

Kids, if you read this, don't try these shenanigans. Since those episodes in Eustis years ago, most of my hair has fallen out!

21

Some Kids Need Two Churches

GREENLEE FAMILY
BARNES AVENUE
1943

Daddy and Mama were of different denominations, he being a Seventh Day Adventist Elder and lay preacher, and she a Sunday School teacher and later the secretary at the First Baptist Church. I reckon that statistics show that marriages like that don't usually last long. Theirs lasted only 53 years, until Dad died, so I guess there is some validity to that.

John, Miriam and I often had a weekend of "religion!" For some years we attended church with Daddy on Saturday and Mama on Sunday. The Seventh Day Adventist church in those days met beside the fire station, right under the Eustis Public Library on Orange Avenue. First Baptist was on the corner of Prescott Street and Orange Avenue. The original building was wooden and located directly across Prescott from the beautiful new brick building that would soon house our congregation.

It must have been in the late 1940s and the new church building was not quite complete. But one Friday evening the old building caught fire! It burnt badly but portions were still usable. However, soon the building caught fire again and that time it burnt nearly to the ground! The church bell that had rung out for years on Sunday mornings in chorus with the ones at the Methodist and Presbyterian churches, would ring no more. They said that it fell through that burning building and made one last loud clang as it hit the ground!

At the time of these fires both the old and the new building were being utilized. Although the new one was not finished, services were being held there. The congregation meeting in the old building moved after the fires to the old Methodist Church building across from Mingonet's Pearl Florists on the corner of Hawley Street and Citrus Avenue.

When completed, the new First Baptist Church was a very beautiful edifice indeed! But, would you believe it, one Sunday night not long after, that new building caught fire too! Great damage was done, and the church met at Eustis High School while it was being repaired. Come to find out that all three of these fires were the work of a young arsonist.

The two pastors that come to mind during my years attending Sunday School, worship and Baptist Training Union are Rev. Marcus Epperson and later Rev. Hoke Shirley.

That "double dose" of religion I got as a youngster stood me good through the years. I reckon God knows who needs just a little bit more! I am thankful to my parents today for that upbringing we children got in the churches.

22

Raymond and His Dental Alteration

If I had an extra dime in my pocket, my walk home from Eustis High School in the early 1950s usually included a trip up the little unpaved alley that is now called East Stevens Street (maybe then, too) that runs between Center and Grove Streets. On this lane was White's Bakery. Lord have mercy, those White's could make great little pies! Apple, blueberry, cherry, all were individually baked and cost a dime.

Another favorite place to stop and spend a little time was H. S. Hunsucker's Service Station on the corner of Grove Street and Palm Avenue. I remember that one of the gas pumps had a handle on the side. You had to pull and push that handle until gasoline was sucked up from the tank underground and into a glass container at the top. There were marks on the sides to let you know how much gas you had up there. Then you would put the nozzle into your gas tank and gravity would put the gas into it. There were also a couple of other pumps that worked with electricity but they were not as much fun to watch.

There was nice candy counter in that service station and a case full of ice water with soft drinks in it. Both Mr. and Mrs. Hunsucker were very friendly to us kids and it was not uncommon to find 4 or 5 of us under their feet in there. My friend Raymond was there one day and he was drinking a Coke. Another older boy was proudly demonstrating his skills at swinging a basketball around holding it in one hand. Just as Raymond took a swig of his drink, the basketball came out of the fella's hand. It hit the end of Raymond's Coke bottle and broke off every tooth in the front his mouth except one upper front tooth! Folks, these were permanent teeth; not baby teeth!

Well, you'da thought he'd gone straight home with this bad news! But no. He wanted me to see it first. So he came to my house on his bike and grinned broadly at me. He really looked funny and I just about croaked! (I think "croaking" is also a good way to describe his dad and mom's reaction later on that day.)

23

The Eustis Junior Fire Department

In the late 1940s, the Eustis Junior Fire Department was housed in a crudely built shed attached to the back of our garage on Barnes Avenue. I can still see the first fire wagon we had. It was a Radio Flyer with a short ladder attached to the side. Also included were a short length of nondescript garden hose, a shovel, and a small tub to contain water for the hand water pump we had. We had a bicycle siren that we rigged so it could be turned by hand in cases of extreme emergency. Noticing our continued interest in our little fire department, Daddy built us a new fire wagon. It was larger, of wood and had a big box on the back in which to put our fire-fighting equipment. It was heavier to push, but we considered it a state-of-the-art machine!

Firefighters included besides myself, brother John, Dale Bartholomew and David Ayers among others. Well, folks, we had a real fire to go to once! A house trailer located on our block had a kitchen fire. Nothing could have suited our young fancies better than that! All that roaring up and down Barnes Avenue, pushing and pulling our fire wagon as we went to make-believe fires, all that practice was finally paying off!

But by the time we had scrambled together behind our garage, got enough water in our tub (filled with our backyard hose – took a while), and dragged that contraption down to the fire a half block away, the Eustis Fire Department had arrived and was already laying out their own *real* fire hoses and equipment. We pulled up with the best of intentions, but before we even had a chance  to get our hand pump a-going, somebody grabbed our tub and threw the water on the fire. Our water was gone in one fell swoop! We were out of business just like that!

I reckon our little tub of water did some good. The fire eventually was quenched and the trailer was saved. But we were one sad little fire department! Our chance to show our stuff had been taken away by a thoughtless act of some grownup, or so we viewed it. Not long afterwards, the Eustis Junior Fire Department stood abandoned as our interests turned to other great ventures.

24

Familiar Voice on Barnes Avenue, and Donkey Baseball

"VEJ-JI-TUH-BULLS", rang out the voice of a well-known figure of our childhood. It was Mr. Burns coming slowly up Barnes Avenue in his pickup truck. He had built a wooden contraption that fit in the back, and it held a number of bins full of produce. It had a little roof over it. You would hear the unmistakable sound of his old truck slowly chugging along. In front of each house he would stop and holler the word "vegetables". I reckon it stuck in my mind because he pronounced distinctly each of the 4 syllables. (Heck, maybe it's really a 3-syllable word and he just gave it a fourth.) Mr. Burns came by through the years in the 1940s and early 1950s. I think he grew his stuff out near Grand Island. He must've done okay, because he kept at it.

We had two sources of milk products that were actually produced in Eustis back in my childhood. They were Simpson's Jersey Dairy and Schneider's Creamery. And classmate Carl Harris' dad owned the Rulon soft drink company for a time. I was sorry when it went out of business as I liked the taste of it. All of those businesses are gone now.

Another thing I remember that was done on occasion was Donkey Baseball. The game had to be played while riding a donkey. I never saw an actual game, but Dick Floyd reminds me that they were played at the Eustis Baseball Park. Sure glad I wasn't on the cleanup crew after the games! I haven't heard of it being played now in years, but it probably is somewhere. Mr. and Mrs. Hammond, our neighbors across Barnes Avenue, owned a large fenced-in lot that covered from their house all the way to Center

Street. On the lot were small scrubby trees of some sort. Well, he allowed the donkey baseball folks to keep their donkeys on that large lot for a while.

We neighborhood kids used to hang around over there some. I usually kept my distance from the donkeys, but on one occasion Janet Bartholomew and I either climbed on or were put on one of them, the latter probably being correct. The donkey took exception to his riders and did a pretty smart thing to get rid of us. And get rid of us he did! He simply walked under a very low hanging limb and scraped us right off! I stayed clear of them after that and I think Janet did too.

25

Yellow Jacket Revenge

I had two boyhood friends named Raymond, so sometimes when I say Raymond I mean Raymond Parrish and at other times I mean Raymond Lang. I am positive that Raymond Lang remembers this day! Brother John, Cousin Richard and I were walking with Daddy on a Saturday afternoon. We had gone down Grove Street and turned up either E. Chesley or E. Dicie Avenue toward Bay Street. There we ran into friend Raymond who lived close by. And that's where we 4 boys came across a nest of yellow jackets (at least that's what I'll call them), coming and going from a hole in the ground! What a great opportunity to harass a bunch of bees!

We began by tossing stones and debris at their hole from a distance, causing momentary disturbances among them. As we became braver, we began to get a running start and jump over their hole. This caused more disorganized disturbance among the yellow jackets that were now angry but restrained. The previous sentence is very important to this story. After another jump, the ground was suddenly covered with these insects, all around their hole! They were obviously waiting for the next "fly-over" by their antagonists!

Even in our youthful exuberance, John, Richard and I realized the folly of taking another jump. But not Raymond. After he questioned our courage, he took off for another jump. What followed was fascinating, painful and instructive. Fascinating for Daddy, John, Richard and me as we saw those yellow jackets rise in concert and in perfect order, to chase Raymond. They were in a V formation with a definite leader.

And painful and instructive to Raymond. After he finally stopped running, he spent a while screaming and crying while Daddy took a pine bough and knocked most of the yellow jackets off of him. He had been stung multiple times from pretty much his top to his bottom! In fact, one of those very angry flying insects even crawled inside his pants through his button-up fly. We all saw it go in! Raymond made a grab and held that portion of his attire in his tightly clinched fist as he tore out for his house!

Well, he came to school on Monday but he looked like a ghost with all of that Calamine Lotion on him. This was about 56 years ago. And I am confident that Raymond has never harassed yellow jackets again through all these years! I know I haven't.

26

Jerry Lloyd and the Honey Bees

A funny incident from probably 1950 or so happened like this: Friend Jerry Lloyd Davis had come to the house and he and I went across Barnes Avenue, into what was a vacant lot at that time. We went over to watch Dale Bartholomew do some things with his two honeybee hives that stood against the fence that surrounded a large citrus grove at the back of the lot. Now, Dale was dressed up in his bee tending garb, you know, with pants tucked into his socks and the like, to keep those varmints out. He also had gloves and a head cover with a screen in it and a smoke-blower in his hand. So he was ready for any eventuality. Not so for Jerry Lloyd and me.

Let's just say I was an interested party from afar, standing back a healthy distance under a scrub oak tree. Well, curiosity got the best of ole Jerry Lloyd, and he got a little too close. Couple this with the fact that the bees were already highly upset with Dale for messing with them. Disaster was approaching! Suddenly Jerry Lloyd started batting the air around his head with both hands and he commenced to running!

I'd always heard that if you get in the shade when a bee is after you, he will leave you alone. So I yelled that information to Jerry Lloyd and invited him under the tree with me. When in his desperation he heard my advice about "shade", the only shade he could see was under a sticker bush in Mrs. Haines' front yard. That low growing bush was probably 100 feet away, so with arms just a-flailing away at that bee (maybe two), Jerry Lloyd headed out for it at full speed! He bypassed my nice shade tree and several others on the way.

The entertainment value of those few moments was priceless for this little boy, and brings smiles even today! Upon reaching the sticker bush, Jerry Lloyd took a headlong dive under it! He emerged only seconds later with a generous load of stickers and a bee sting! Looking back, maybe its good he didn't join me in my shade. There might have been two of us stung.

27

Miriam and her Improvised Car-Entry

It was a great way to make a few dollars in 1951! We guys would deliver handbills for Jason's Groceteria after school. Most of these advertisements are mailed out today or come in the newspapers, but not then. Jimmy Cincogranni who worked at Jason's would take us out to far away areas and drop us off. Then we'd go house to house with those ad sheets, and would meet Jimmy at a pick up point.

Well, Daddy decided that it would be nice if he too designed a handbill advertising the things he had to offer at Greenlee's Shoe Shop, like half soles, heels, shoe polish and the like. We Greenlee kids were conscripted to deliver these handbills.

So Mama had taken us way out Lakeview Avenue and down East Crooked Lake Drive. She was driving slowly along while we kids were going to the houses with the handbills. I have told you all this to set up another incident that I would pay admission to see again.

On Miriam's side of the street lived another Jimmy, a school classmate that she was sweet on. (I don't know if he knew this or not… Maybe I am breaking news here!) She was excited to be able to go to his house and deliver the handbill. Who knows? Maybe he would be there! Well, she got to his door, and when no one answered her knock, she left the handbill and started back to the car. At that moment, a great big dog roared around the corner of the house in full barking mode!

Miriam came flying up that sidewalk and made one of the finest dives I had seen up to then! That 12-year-old girl dove through the driver's side window of that 1937 Chevy, right across in front of her startled Mama! A little more than half of her made it into the car. What remained protruding from the window I will leave to your imagination. It protruded until Mama drove a short distance and the dog went home. It's probably good that Jimmy wasn't around. (You never have your Brownie Hawkeye camera when you need it!)

28

Adventures at Waterman Memorial Hospital

The Waterman Memorial Hospital was located in the Fountain Inn Hotel, the largest building in town, and it was fronted by Magnolia Avenue and the two sides were on Grove and Eustis Streets. I know that building is no more and the hospital is on Highway 441 now. But in the early 1950s, several of my friends had jobs there running the elevator. I reckon there were 4, maybe 5 floors to that building.

The elevator was put in motion by a lever that the operator would toggle back and forth. The trick was knowing when to let go of the lever so it would stop pretty near the level of the floor, or else the rider would have to step up or down. Once stopped, the operator would have to open a gate in the elevator and then the door.

Once in awhile I would get to operate that thing when Bill or another friend would be on break. It was fun but also embarrassing to have to tell folks to "please step up (or down)". I never did get the hang of stopping it right at floor level! People were nice, though, and never complained.

Once my friend Tommy was in that hospital for an appendectomy. Now, Tommy was a live wire. He was a good boy but not above a little mischief sometimes like a few others I knew. It was very shortly after surgery that he was wheeling himself up and down the long halls of that place. Over the doors of the patient's rooms there were big fans to circulate the air. (There was no air conditioning there in those days.) Tommy discovered that you could take a handful of wet toilet paper and toss it into one of those running fans, and the result would be a sprinkling of tiny bits of toilet paper, raining down all over a patient's room! Patients and hospital staff alike were not amused by this practice. Tommy just might have been sent home a little early.

Dr. Louis R. Bowen was our family doctor. His son Dickie was in our class, and his brother Bobby a year behind us. I remember also Dr. Williams and Dr. Tyre who among others, were practicing in my childhood. Eustis was blessed to have great medical facilities and doctors.

29

My Embarrassment
at the State Theatre

Although we always wanted to, our parents thought it was best that we children not go to the movie theatre. No Golden Movie Garden and no State Theatre. For the young years of our lives we had to find other ways to amuse ourselves, and we did. But the time finally came when Mama and Daddy decided that we could go to the Saturday night shows. I must've been in the 7th grade at that time, say 1950.

It didn't really matter much what was showing (everything was fit to be seen in those days), we kids were usually there. The balcony in the State Theatre was always stuffed to the gills with teens, with all the accompanying whispering, laughing, arguing, and articles being tossed about. Somehow we managed to even watch a little of the show sometimes.

One Saturday night Harold Webb and I were pacing back and forth at the top of the balcony, looking over the crowd. Actually, it was at about this time that both of us were beginning to notice the girls, and we were pointing out certain ones and commenting on them to each other.

Suddenly, I laid my eyes on a most beautiful head of blonde hair! I excitedly pointed her out to Harold, and neither of us could identify her from the back. It was decided that since I had spotted her first, I would be the one to find out who she was. Well, I was still too shy at this point to walk down to her row for a better look. But there was another avenue available to me: Throw something at her and make her turn around!

So I deftly tore the top off my popcorn box and wadded it into a tight ball. And with Harold looking on with rapt attention, I threw my "missile of love" right into the back of her beautiful blonde head! What happened next set my social life back another good three years! That girl spun her head around, and yelled, "Jamie, stop it!" To my eternal embarrassment and Harold's absolute delight, I had made a pass at my sister, Miriam!

It was another night that some of us guys had been to a scary late movie, and I had to walk home alone. Well, I was a big 13-year-old, so that would be no big deal. Grove Street was well lighted...*except on that night*! There was a power outage all the way down that street! No house lights, no street lights and no moon! It was absolutely pitch dark! That walk turned into a big deal fast! Walking briskly in the middle of Grove Street, I got down to where Ward Avenue intersects, where the Church of God and The Gas Well service station were located.

I was so sure somebody was coming to get me from that gloomy gas station, that I balled up my fists and shouted "Come get me!" Then I tore out for Barnes Avenue as fast as my short legs could carry me!

It's a right good run from Ward Avenue to Barnes Avenue for a well-trained athlete, which I wasn't. I didn't meet one car in that midnight hour as I raced up the middle of Grove Street! Barnes Avenue never looked so good to me! Reckon I used up about a quart of adrenaline!

30

World War II Watchtower Volunteers

In some of my articles, I have written about some happenings in Eustis that I remember from the days of World War II. These references elicited some comments from a few who shared childhood with me. They told me of the watchtower that had stood in Ferran Park during the war. That I do not remember. I asked my brother John who is a year older than me, and he said that though he remembers several watchtowers around, he does not remember that one either.

Dick Floyd wrote: "Remember the old watchtower that was in the Park? Dad bought it after the war for $25.00 and we tore it down. Used the lumber to build a garage at the house on Ward Avenue." Ruby Wanland added this: "My Mom and Dad volunteered to take turns watching for aircraft down at Ferran Park. They had a tower there and they were to call Orlando to identify any and all aircraft. All this was at night after they had worked all day. My Dad ran the A & P store."

Bob Andrews sent his comments to his brother Bill who forwarded me this: "Just the mention of the watchtower brings back memories. I was a watcher, matched with a man whose name I don't remember…it was mostly at night…my older friend was a veteran of WWI, where he lost a leg. I remember calling in a spot, don't know where the call went, but it obviously was a dedicated line. A half hour later I called in another spot, and was questioned by the woman operator at the other end, asking me if I was sure it wasn't a plane circling! I was about a teen or close to a teen at the time, and received a pin for civilian air watch. Wish I still had it."

31

Memories of Downtown Eustis

Sometime in the late 1940s, Mama left substitute teaching and became a sales clerk at Ferran's Department Store on Magnolia Avenue. Yes, I walked on those squeaky floors in that place many times. I recall an early record player of some sort that sat next to a pillar in the front part of the store. It played a huge metal record that would slowly turn if you cranked it a few times. Ferran's is gone now and a restaurant is located in the building.

When in town during Christmas of 2005, I had lunch with a group of 1955'ers in there. And Sandy (Craft) Clark asked if anyone remembered that record player! I had just been thinking about it, and was glad to know that we shared that memory.

The Eustis Public Library on the corner of Orange Avenue and Grove Street was another place I liked to visit, but it wasn't because of the great books on hand there. Two things grabbed my attention. First, there was a stuffed armadillo sitting in the back of the library on a bookcase. In those days, armadillos were a rarity at least to me, and I marveled at his armor. Sometime later armadillos became common in central Florida, and rivaled the possum as King of the Road-Kill department.

The other interesting item in that library for me was the forerunner of the ViewMaster I reckon, a wooden gadget called a Stereopticon. You'd slip a double print of the same picture in a little wire holder and slide it up the stick while looking through the eyepieces, and when it was focused you had a 3-D image of it. That was the first 3-dimension picture experience of my life! Fascinating!

Next time you are in the library, see if they still have the Stereopticon. Show your kids how it used to be.

32

Remembering Sports Stars of High School

I played baseball in high school with some limited success. If desire had anything to do with being a great baseball player I would have been tops. I reckon I was just adequate, and did stay on the team. But I was surrounded by some very good players. One I single out as having the greatest natural talent of any of them, at least in my opinion, was Harold Webb. Harold had all of the tools and I got a kick out of just watching him do his thing! He raised the interest of some major league scouts and even went to a summer camp for the Baltimore Orioles after graduation, but I reckon he opted to do other things with his life. Shoot, I'd have crawled on my hands and knees all the way to Boston if I could have played for the Red Sox!

Another great athlete was David Ayers. He was a starting pitcher on the baseball team and the starting quarterback on the football team in my high school years. Our teams would have had a hard time without him. Many of my close friends played on the football team. One unique character was Hal Purvis. Hal sometimes used a method of tackling that was different but quite effective. As a runner would come his way, he would duck away like he was trying to avoid any contact. Then as fast as lightning, he would reach one hand out and grab the runner's foot as he passed. Within a couple of yards that runner would come down like he was in a train wreck!

Basketball was played in my childhood and in my early teens in the old wooden gymnasium building on the corner of Bay Street and Woodward Avenue. Several of the players that I recall from the various teams are Freddy and Bobby Belton, Jack Temple, "Squeaky" Hammond and Alton

Crawford. But that old gym was an eyesore and looked like it had never had a coat of paint! It was finally torn down. The Armory building was built on that property and the basketball team played there for several years.

The closest place to bowl was in Leesburg. Of course in those days the pins were set manually, at least in little alleys like that one. One thing to remember on manual pin sets is to allow the "setter" to get out of the pit before you bowl again. I hit a pin boy one time, and I thought we were going to have fisticuffs over it. Scared the heck out of me! I bowled with more care after that.

Then there was the Eustis Skating Rink on Highway 19 just out of town toward Mount Dora. I liked the music, but did not do much skating. I had trouble enough keeping my two feet under me and had even less luck trying to stay up on 8 little wheels. But the rink was quite the hang out, too.

33

The Junior United States Marine Corps: Defenders of Freedom

I'm not sure what sparked my interest in the military, unless it was my Uncle Buddy who was in the Second World War. But just as the Eustis Junior Fire Department was at our home address, so was the Junior United States Marine Corps. It was headquartered in our basement. On the concrete wall at the bottom of the outside stairs right by the door, a roughly painted sign read: J. U. S. M. C. NO GIRLS ALLOWED. (It would be a few more years before any of us thought that having girls around might be a good idea.) We boys in the neighborhood were ready for action!

One of us had a BB gun, canteen and belt. Another had a backpack and the other had a helmet of World War I vintage. We would take turns dressing up one of us in all of the equipment. We never fought in a real conflict but we were always ready if one came along.

I was 13 in 1950 when the war in Korea began. And it was a conflict far larger than the Junior United States Marine Corps could handle. But again, I took what I reckon was a rather uncommon interest for a kid my age in war that involved us. Every day the Tampa Tribune that was delivered to our house had a little map of the Korean peninsula showing where the enemy was and where we were. I cut out each of these maps and pored over them. I watched with great concern as the territory we held got smaller and smaller down at the bottom of South Korea near Fusan, and thought for sure that the end was near and that we were going to be pushed into the sea.

But then General Douglas MacArthur ordered the landing of the marines at Inchon. It was a surprise move, and we got that 2nd front going real fast as our troops closed the pinchers on an enemy now trapped between our two fronts. I was absolutely ecstatic! My little pile of maps was growing and the news looked better every day. I refer to "us" and "we" when I mention the troops in that war. Although there were other forces under the UN flag there, as usual the fighting forces were comprised of mostly us. This little Eustis boy was very proud of those troops and the United States!

After the war had come to a shaky ending at the 38th parallel in 1953, I kept my formidable stack of maps. However, after I left for the Air Force in 1955, they were unwittingly thrown away! So much for my day-to-day history of the Korean War.

34

Incredible Journey with Bill – Number One

One of the more adventuresome friends I had was Bill Andrews. We had known each other from early childhood when we attended First Baptist Church, and we went through all of our grades in school together and even joined the Air Force together, along with Dick Floyd and Alton Crawford.

Bill was the one to do things "out of the ordinary". While high adventure for me was, for instance, riding my bike the 4 miles to Mount Dora, Bill's idea was to ride to Daytona Beach! Daytona Beach? That was 55 miles away! Well, folks, that's exactly what we did. I reckon we were 10th graders or so. Bill had access to two 3-speed bicycles and a brother with a houseboat in the Halifax River at Daytona. That was all we needed. We would simply ride over and spend the night on that boat, and return the next day. Easy enough? Lord have mercy, we did it, but I vowed I'd never try that again!

We went out Orange Avenue and traveled on the Deland road through Cassia. Between Cassia and the St. John's River is a verrrrry long stretch of Highway 44. In a car it takes a while. On a bike it is interminable! But we finally made the river and then into downtown Deland. I'd never been that far from home on a bike! Thoughts of turning for home sounded pretty good to me, but, hey, we were adventurers!

So, we got on Highway 92 out of Deland toward Daytona, and folks, that stretch of road was a bear on my tired legs. Bill didn't say much about it, but I knew he was tired, too. He was probably thinking, "Who's idea was this anyway?" Well, we finally got to Daytona and the Halifax River and the boat. I don't remember much about the boat, but I think I slept real good that night.

So there we were 55 miles away from home, and our little bit of money had dwindled to about zip. But we started for home. To while away the miles we would get those bikes going as fast as we could and then coast to see how many squares of concrete highway we could cover before we stopped. That helped some. But with energy levels running near zero in our bodies, we realized that we had money for only one Pepsi. So we shared it at Deland. Then it was time for that long stretch of Highway 44 again.

Near Cassia we were so hungry that we stopped at a bean patch and picked a few string beans to eat. Then we came to an orange tree and picked a couple of oranges. Folks, Eustis never looked so good to two tired, hungry and thirsty boys coming in on Orange Avenue! That was 110 miles in two days. After that, I'll bet I haven't ridden a bicycle another 110 miles total in the rest of my life up to now.

35

Daddy's Ingenious "Christmas Wheel"

In the mid-1940s, Greenlee's Shoe Shop was still out on Eustis Street next to Bennett's Grocery Store and across the street from Strong's Sporting Goods, when Daddy began to put a "Christmas Wheel" in his shop window. The first ones I remember were disc shaped and probably 4 feet in diameter. On this "Wheel" ran a train made out of little milk cans that was held stationery by a wire while the wheel turned. He had cleverly fashioned a little train engine, coal car and caboose with wheels that rolled. He had painted a track on the Wheel and the train traveled on it through a varied landscape as the Christmas Wheel slowly turned. He sold advertising by painting little billboard signs with the names of companies in Eustis, five dollars a sign. It was well done and drew quite an audience!

When Daddy moved his shop into the Post Office Arcade, he changed the shape of the Wheel. His new one was vertical instead of horizontal. This one would make Rube Goldberg take notice! It was an open sided cylinder again about 4 feet or so in diameter and probably two feet wide. The milk can train was still the star of the show, but it was now controlled by a magnet beneath the surface that was moved by an arm controlled by some device Daddy cooked up. Now the train followed a crooked track. And as the Wheel turned, the season would change from summer to winter and back to summer.

Daddy fixed it so that it would actually snow on the "winter" side of the Wheel! He had devised an overhead tank with holes in it, hidden from view. It contained artificial snow. The tank would turn when the Wheel got to the winter side that was covered with cotton snow. Snow would sprinkle down all over that part of the Wheel! He fixed it so that the tank would be refilled automatically! He rigged a container that the snow would fall into when the winter side was down. Then an electric fan would come on and blow that snow through a tube that took it back up to the tank, ready for next time!

Along with the many advertising signs that graced the Wheel, Daddy had installed a little lake made out of a mirror, and a tiny boat with a little fisherman in it. When the lake was at the top, a trip wire on the inner workings of the Wheel would make the fisherman's fishing pole jerk up like he had caught something!

People would be standing two or three deep watching this Christmas Wheel contraption do its thing! He had the Wheel until he closed Greenlee's Shoe Shop in 1952. I regret that I do not have a picture of the Christmas Wheel.

36

Of Fairs and Fireworks

Really exciting for me was the Lake County Fair at the Eustis Fairgrounds each year. I know that most kids my age in the 1940s and early 50s cared mostly for the midway where the rides and sideshows were. (I know they still do.) But I thoroughly enjoyed walking into the exhibit halls. It was like entering a strange new world. Even the fragrance in the air was different than outside. Seems like I can smell it now. People were enticing you to stop and look at their exhibits. I found them very interesting.

And I liked going through the livestock exhibit, too, and seeing whose rabbit, or pig or calf had won the blue ribbon. (Yeh, I can still smell it too.) And then it was on to the midway to see how many rides I could squeeze out of the limited funds I had. I made sure that I rode the Octopus, the Ferris Wheel and the Tilt-a-Whirl before I was financially depleted.

I remember going to some fireworks at the Fairgrounds one time. Dale Bartholomew was there with us, and though just a year or two older than we were, he had volunteered or had been asked by the town to help them watch for falling embers from the ignited fireworks. Poor Dale didn't get to see any of those beautiful and exciting fireworks do their thing! While we were ooohing and aaahing over them, a very serious-faced Dale was facing the other way dutifully watching the falling sparks. Seems he was wearing something identifying him as a fire warden and he had an extinguisher of some sort. He must have done a good job because we got through the evening without a fire starting.

One of the pleasures our little family had was attending the Tampa Fair each year. We'd load up early in the morning before sunrise and head out for Tampa. Now, if I thought the fair in Eustis was great, that Tampa Fair was magnificent! Many more exhibits and a seemingly unending midway! We hated to leave and would get home very late at night.

Write to you again "fair-ly" soon.

37

Race Cars and Clay Pit Fun

Out just about across the street from the Eustis Baseball Park on West Charlotte Avenue was a place where little cars were raced. This racetrack was located on the edge of the Eustis Airport. The cars were only a couple of feet long with little souped-up motors and they zoomed around a concrete ring while tethered to a pole in the middle of the circle. They made a heck of a racket, and could get up to some pretty good speed. I can still smell the exhaust fumes from the kind of fuel they used. We could hear them racing from our house on Barnes Avenue. It was entertaining and as I recall it was free admission.

The Eustis Airport itself was in business in my early childhood and I think it had closed by the time I graduated from Eustis High in 1955. In my memory, it was bordered in those days by Morin Street to the east, Atwater Avenue on the north, Kurt Street on the west and W. Charlotte Avenue on the south. That was quite a large piece of land and easily took care of the small plane traffic coming to and from Eustis.

I remember a terrible plane crash that took place there one time. I reckon it was a Piper Cub or some such small plane that had two Eustis businessmen in it. Reports said that on takeoff they experienced some kind of motor trouble, and while still at a very low altitude, the pilot elected to try to turn around and come back in to the airport. On banking to turn around with little air speed, the plane simply slid out of the air and crashed. Seems it came down in the Eustis Baseball Park, across the street from the airport.

And then there was the old clay pit where we used to play. We would turn off Taylor Avenue going in to Eustis Heights, onto what is now called Pine

Grove Road. That road was made of clay then. We had much fun roaming that clay pit! It was also used as the city dump (I don't know if officially so), and there were a number of treasures for us boys to find there. Once I found a pair of baseball shoes that fit me pretty good. Baseball shoes were a luxury my family couldn't afford. The cleats on these were almost worn off, but I used them through my high school baseball years. I guarantee that they were ready to return to the dump when I finished with them.

38

"Soup" and the Spider

Daddy was a super practical joker! He was real good at making things with his hands. One time he concocted the ugliest spider you ever saw! It was huge, had springy, hairy legs and was a fearsome-looking creature indeed! He went to great lengths to get up to his high ceiling in his shoe shop in the Post Office Arcade, and install two eyelets, one over his shop door and the other behind his counter. Through these eyelets he ran a thread with the spider attached to the end over the door. He had the other end where he could reach it when he needed to.

He told us that one day a business man in town whose nickname was "Soup", stopped by the shop to pass a pleasantry or two. Lord have mercy, he was standing right in that doorway, with a rolled up newspaper under his arm. What a great time to put the spider to work!

So while Daddy kept Soup engaged in conversation, that spider was being let slooooowly down right in front of him. Suddenly, in mid-sentence, the spider was waving his hairy legs at Soup, about two feet in front of him! Soup froze in place for a moment, then slowly pulled the newspaper out from under his arm, and gave that spider a sudden swat that sent it careening all the way up to that high ceiling! Daddy just about collapsed with laughter. Soup, however, saw nothing funny in the prank! He just picked up the conversation where he had left off like nothing had happened.

I think Daddy was right embarrassed at how that one turned out, but it didn't stop him. He foisted his brand of harmless humor off on his friends, his family, the Post Office and his church. In spite of these things and perhaps sometimes because of them, Daddy was a popular man and well-loved by all who knew him. I was blest to have had him as my father.

39

Eustis Business District of the Early 1950s

A few of these businesses I am going to list come from some pretty deep shadows of my mind. Some I haven't thought of in years. A few might still be in business in Eustis downtown and a few might have moved to outlying shopping centers now. But a great many are gone since the 1940s and 50s. Some readers might well remember others that I have forgotten altogether. Mine is certainly not a comprehensive list!

I know that Merry Jewelers is still thriving in downtown Eustis. My friends and I stopped in to see Smiley Merry back in December of 2005 and again in 2006. Also The Shoe Hospital and the Palm Pharmacy are where I remember them, among others. Mama worked at Ferran's Department Store after she stopped substitute teaching at Eustis Elementary School. Later she worked for Hobbs & Nelson Jewelers and then at Harper's Clothing Store. These three stores were on Magnolia Avenue and are no more.

Other businesses that come to mind that were on Bay Street from the 1940s and early 1950s are Ashford Electric, A. D. & C. D. Miller Hardware, B. E. Thompson Furniture, Shorty's Taxi, some liquor store and pool room, the State Theatre, Bay Street Pharmacy, Igou's Farm Store, Polk Buick, Pugh's Dry Cleaners, Branton's Grocery, Jennings Rou Packing House, LuDell's Bar, and others that I can picture but cannot put a name with them. There were also at least four car dealerships or used car lots, the Ford place and the Chrysler-Plymouth place, both in the downtown area.

Farther out were the Chevrolet dealership and another lot next to Branton's Grocery. Maybe that was the Pontiac dealership.

Businesses beside those I named before from Magnolia were Porters' Photography, Western Auto, Jason's Groceteria, First State Bank, Florida Power Co, Eberhardt's Candy Store, Church's Jewelry, Storey's Grocery Store, Waterman Memorial Hospital, City Hall Building that later was radio station WEUS studio for a while, Brown's Hardware, Firestone, and McCrory's 5 & 10 Cent Store. I know I'm skipping many! Orange Avenue had Ayer's Radio and TV, Gauss Radio Shop, and a hardware store on the other side of the street.

From Eustis Street, among others, were Strong's Sporting Goods, Bennett's Grocery Store, Brown's Hardware, Greenlee's Shoe Shop (first on Eustis Street and then in the Post Office Arcade), Dollar's Fish Market, Brady's Dress Shop, Coursey's Dry Cleaners, the Eustis Telephone Exchange, and Dr.Clift's Chiropractic Clinic.

On Grove Street I remember Marshall's Bicycle Repair Shop, the A&P Store, as well as another grocery store across from the City Hall, and the Grand View Hotel on the corner of Grove and Magnolia. And of course, The Gas Well and Hunsucker's Service Station.

Also, I remember two flower shops, Bishop's downtown and Mingonet's Pearl Florists on Citrus Avenue. And LaRoe's Machine Shop out Orange Avenue comes to mind. This article could go on and on, but I just wanted to bring some of these business names to our remembrance.

I remember Eustis as having a thriving downtown business in those days before the mega shopping centers came along. I am happy to see that some of the old standbys as well as the new businesses in downtown are maintaining a shopping area to be proud of!

40

Incredible Journey with Bill – Number Two

Here goes Bill Andrews and me off on another adventure! Do you know that you can get all the way to Silver Springs by water from Lake Eustis? Bill knew that. I didn't. So this was to be a 4-day camping trip to Silver Springs! Again, we were pretty young to be off by ourselves like this, but our parents gave us permission. So we packed our stuff and put his boat into Lake Eustis and were away!

After crossing the lake we entered Haines Creek (renamed Haynes Creek in 1995 to correct an old error) at Grand Island. Up the creek we went and then into Lake Griffin. I remember the lake being quite filled with hyacinths but there was a lane for us to get through. Then we entered the Ocklawaha River. We turned and wound around a bit, and in a few hours we reached the spot where the Ocklawaha meets Silver River, or Silver Run as we called it then.

We turned up Silver Run toward Silver Springs, and just below the Springs we pulled over and set up camp on the edge of a cow pasture. We spent our time doing a lot of swimming in that cold river and eating. I even killed a large snake with a machete. Several times we went up a little closer to the Springs and climbed into a large tree that hung over the river. Those excursion boats, crowded with visitors, would come down and pass where we were. We were set for them.

As they got near we would hear the guide say over his sound system, "Well, look up ahead, folks. There's a couple of little Tarzan's up in the tree!" That was Bill's cue. Now, he could dive with the best of them, and out of that tree he would do a fancy gainer and a half with a full body twist in the pike position (don't know what I just described, but anyhow his dives were entertaining.) My dives were more like somebody shoving a refrigerator into the river.

Well, the folks would whistle and clap and throw coins into the river for us. That was okay, because we could see them on the bottom, as the water was crystal clear! On our last day, we went right into Silver Springs proper, got out of the boat and walked some distance to an "Orange Juice! All-You-Can-Drink-For-10 Cents!" stand.

Now Bill and I both like orange juice. I mean really like it! But our time of liquid refreshment turned into a drinking contest. We plunked down our dime apiece and commenced to empty glass after glass. This did not set well with the operator of the stand. I can't blame him, but I won the contest. I drank 9 glasses and Bill stopped with 8. (He may remember the outcome differently.) Folks, that's 17 glasses of orange juice for 20 cents! As we waddled away from the place, that operator dismissed us with some snide remark. I think it had to do with us not coming back.

I want to mention something I found very interesting. The Ocklawaha River is brown and muddy- looking. Where Silver Run meets it with its sparkling clear water, the two rivers flow together for a while, with one side of the river very clear and the other very dark. But after several hundred yards the rivers blend with each other, and become one dark brown river. There is a theological point to be made about this occurrence, and I'll bet you know what it is.

41

Camphor Berry Baseball

Bet you never played camphor berry baseball! Major League Camphor Berry Baseball! One of my fond memories from the early 1950s took place on a regular basis at the ballpark in our front yard. This park consisted of our sidewalk and our front screen door. We had two camphor trees, one on either side of the sidewalk. When the berries were green and hard, it was game time!

Here's how it went. We would throw the berries at the screen door from the end of the sidewalk. If we hit the screen itself, it was a strike. If the berry hit the wood part of the door, it was a hit. Anywhere else the berry hit, it was a ball.

Alton Crawford was the "Brooklyn Dodgers" and I was the "Boston Red Sox." He was usually Don Newcombe, the great Dodger pitcher, or maybe Carl Erskine. I was most always Mel Parnell, the Boston great lefthander. Sometimes I would be Ellis Kinder, the Boston fine relief pitcher.

We learned that if you take the berry and roll it between your middle finger and thumb as you throw it, it will curve. Actually, we became pretty skilled at tossing those berries! Folks, we had some bodacious 9-inning games there! Alton has gone to be with the Lord now, but if he was still around and the present owner of my boyhood house on Barnes Avenue was okay with it, I would love to play against him again. I haven't forgotten how to toss the berry!

Another thing we liked to do was to hit gravel rocks with a broomstick. We got quite adept at smacking them from Barnes Avenue over in to the orange grove, probably 50 yards or so away. One hit over the fence that surrounded the grove was a home run. I reckon you master anything you do often enough. And there was an endless supply of rocks on unpaved but graveled Barnes Avenue.

Check with you "berry" soon again.

42

Golf Ball Find and Disposal

The long-closed Eustis Golf and Country Club was at the top of the hill on Country Club Road. It had been defunct for a number of years when several of us young teens went tramping around the old course. We came upon a small pond adjacent to one of the overgrown fairways. I was told that it was called "Lake Dammit" by the golfers who had played that course. (Today I can well understand what they meant.)

Well, we took our shoes off and started wading around in the shallow water. And…what was that I stepped on? A golf ball! Down under the muck that squeezed up between my toes there was a golf ball! And not only that one! They were all over the place under that layer of muck! Been down there for years!

We got a sack and begin to fish those balls out of Lake Dammit. After a while we had quite a sack full. And I ended up with ownership of them all. Now, I knew nothing about golf (which is only slightly less than I know now), but a sack full of treasure like that was not intended to just sit around in the corner of my bedroom forever! And folks, I did own a baseball bat. So I took those balls with me into the middle of Barnes Avenue, and commenced to smackin' them out into the orange grove across the street from our house.

Do you know how far a well-hit golf ball will go when struck with a baseball bat? Lord have mercy, it'll go on forever! Suddenly I was Ted Williams (Boston Red Sox leftfielder) hitting these tremendous home runs! There's more to this story…

Our long-suffering neighbor had a very large, rusty looking metal building behind her house, beyond her guava bushes and her chicken yard. The building had a tin roof. Well, let's just say that one of my home run swings sent a golf ball into "fowl" territory! That ball climbed into the sky over the chicken yard and by my calculations, it would finally come to rest on that building's big tin roof!

I kid you not, that ball was so well hit that I had time to grab my bat and bag of golf balls, and run pretty near to the backyard of my house before Mr. Ball met Mr. Tin Roof! BAM! Then it bounced way up in the air and came down again… BAM!… BAM!… Bam.. Bam.. bam. Folks, you could have heard that noise clear over on Atwater Avenue, a block away! From my vantage point I could see our neighbor moving with haste into her back yard. But the source of that noise remained a mystery that only one of us knew the answer to, at least until you folks read this.

43

Ants in Pants; Multiple Earthworm Ingestion

In the early 1950s many of us guys took Agriculture in school. Dixie Driggers was our Ag teacher. The class had a plot of land over on McDonald Avenue, where we grew a lot of vegetables. I reckon it was for practice, but I know that some of them went to the grocery stores in Eustis.

Several events come to mind from that place. A couple of the guys were trying to get an old fence post out of the ground, and a bunch of big ants came up from around it. One of those varmints went straight up friend Jim Moore's pants leg! We were treated to the first – and probably the last – incident of indecent exposure at that vegetable garden, as Jim quickly got down to bare essentials in pursuit of that ant! A maverick ant'll do that for you, folks.

Another event remains quite fresh in my mind. This garden was the place where I first swallowed an earthworm on purpose. In digging around and getting the ground ready to plant something, I came across a fairly large worm. I was displaying my find when talk began amongst the guys about what it would take to get me to eat that worm!

I didn't take the chatter serious until one fella offered me a quarter, and another upped the offer to include an unopened 5-stick pack of gum. I reckon I was pretty easy, because I decided to go with that offer!

This is how I did it: I worked up a big mouthful of spit. Tilting my head back and opening my mouth real wide, I dropped that hapless worm right in there. One big swallow and he was gone!

Well, that was a big status builder! That feat brought a modicum of short-lived respect from my fellow "future farmers" there, and I pocketed the quarter and 4 sticks of gum! Remember I said it was where I <u>first</u> swallowed an earthworm on purpose? There was a second time.

That very afternoon I had gone over to Harold Webb's house and there I boasted of my earlier feat. He accused me of telling him an untruth. Sooooo, out we went to his backyard and under the faucet we dug around a little until we found another earthworm. Right. I did it again. Made a believer out of him. Thank the Lord, I also learned that you don't have to go around proving yourself over and over again like that. No more ingesting worms on purpose.

Mr. Driggers asked me if I would pick the okra during the time school was out. I was to fill a bushel hamper or basket and take it to Jason's Groceteria downtown once a week. I don't remember the compensation, but they don't print enough money for me to do that again! I would ride my bike from Barnes Avenue all the way out McDonald Avenue extension to the vegetable field, pick that okra until my back almost broke, and carry that huge basket on my handlebars to town, actually pushing the bike most of the way. I was never so glad to see school start again! And it took a lot for me to make the preceding statement!

44

Senior Skip Day

Senior Skip Day was great fun for me! Instead of studies on that day, off to Daytona Beach we went, almost everyone in the class! I remember that it was a cloudy day and really not all that hot. Perfect for me, because I am fair-skinned and burn easily. There would be no problems on that day!

We horsed around on that beach for the better part of the day, and me with no sunscreen on. Who needs sunscreen on a cloudy day? It was getting along toward late afternoon and the guys and gals around me begin to notice and told me that I looked pretty red. And I guess my skin did sort of feel a little tight and funny. Lord have mercy, by the time we got on that yellow school bus, I was flaming red and beginning to blister!

Now, I've had some record-breaking sunburns in my day, and I rank that one solidly in second place! The only person worse off than me that I knew about that day was Bill. He was so sunburned that he got sick and had to ride home in a grade mother's car.

Folks, I was a little shy around the girls. I didn't date and so I went to the Prom alone. And I felt pretty uncomfortable while there, but there were a few other guys who didn't have dates either. So we kinda hung together. But I did enjoy going to the beach early on the morning after the prom.

I was riding in a car full of guys going toward Cassia on the way again to Daytona. Suddenly we hit a pocket of fog – the thickest fog I have ever seen to this day! Zero visibility! That's the kind of fog where these great big car pileups take place. I reckon we were spared being hit because traffic through Cassia at 5 a.m. in those days was sparse indeed. We stopped and one of us got out and walked along the edge of the road with his hand on the right front fender. We crept along at his walking pace until finally coming out the other side of that fog. It might have been a quarter of a mile!

I don't remember too much about that trip other than I picked up another bad sunburn. Reckon I didn't learn too much from the Skip Day trip. Because of my escapades with the sun throughout my childhood and teen years, my dermatologist here in North Carolina is living in luxury!

Wear your sunscreen, kids, and keep your dermatologist humble!

45

Motorized Two-Wheeler Troubles

Raymond Parrish's brother had a very nice motorcycle, a big one! Now, in the early 1950s we boys were several years too young to be operating motor vehicles. Well, Raymond "borrowed" that fine bike one day and two of us guys rode it with him. Can't remember who the other buddy was. Why it always seemed to be me, I don't know, but the seat had room for only two people. So I was the one selected to ride on the back fender and hang on around my buddy's waist.

Folks, that back fender was made of smooth metal that curved rather closely to the configuration of the back wheel. That fact plays into this episode. We made it okay from the corner of Eustis Street and Atwater Avenue where Raymond lived, up to Grove Street. To that point I rather enjoyed it. (But you can't really get up too much speed in that short block there.)

Raymond turned on to Grove, heading south toward the Old Mount Dora Road. And right away things went "south" for me, too! We were almost immediately traveling at an excessive rate of speed! And with every bump we hit, my seat on the back fender was becoming less secure! I said I don't remember who the other boy was, but I really should. Anybody I'd hugged around the waist that tightly you'd think I would remember! But still I was sliding down that fender little by little! I was hollering with all my considerable voice, but the noise of the motorcycle and the rush of the wind drowned me out!

I had about decided that I had had it, and was wondering just how much fender was remaining below my sliding rear end! Providence stepped in at this point. Raymond had reached the Old Mount Dora Road, and he had to slow way down to turn! That's when I was able to make myself heard! Friends, I got off that motorcycle and walked back to Barnes Avenue, thanking God with every step!

One evening Charlie Smith, a friend of both John's and mine, had come to the house on his Cushman Eagle motorbike. Though I still did not have a license, I asked Charlie if I could take a ride on it. I rode it to the Dairy Freeze on Bay Street. Some of the other young teens were standing around admiring it, when one of Eustis' Finest stopped by. Coulda been Dick Shirk, I just don't remember. But I do remember sweating it out while he came over and looked at the Eagle, too. I just knew that sooner or later he would ask who was riding it. But he never did. Shortly thereafter I "legalized" myself by getting my driver's license.

46

Boat Stuff

Why was it that so many of my childhood episodes of "high adventure" include Bill Andrews?

Here's another one: There's nuthin' like skimming over the water at break neck speed as one is bouncing and being slapped in the stomach while lying face down on the front of a hydroplane, hanging on for dear life! I know that, because in the early 1950s, Bill and I rode on more than one occasion across and round about Lake Eustis in such fashion. I can still hear him laughing with delight as he swerved that craft while I wondered at my sanity for agreeing to ride in that precarious position! Note that I said "on more than one occasion," so I reckon that answers the sanity thing.

Seems Bill delighted in going back across his own wake at full speed (which was considerable) just to see if he could make my grip become less secure! Well, I never went off, but I had the whitest knuckles of any kid I knew! For a young guy who was not anxious to attempt a swim to shore from way out on that big lake, I seemed to enjoy "living on the edge!" We both survived those teen years and remained the closest of friends until he went to be with the Lord in 2012.

It must have been about 1953 when some of us guys found a rickety rowboat adrift on West Crooked Lake. We claimed ownership using the "law of the sea" (at least one of us had heard that there was such a law). We had fun rowing that thing around. But I remember one terrifying incident, at least for me. I knew that my brother John and a friend Hal Purvis had gone down to the lake to take the boat out. The hour had gotten late and Mama had sent me down there to fetch John.

When I arrived at the lake, I saw the boat upside-down and probably 200 feet from shore! The boys were nowhere to be seen! Friends, my heart froze as I assumed a tragedy must have occurred. I beat it home as fast as my bicycle could go! How was I going to break this news to Mama?

When I skidded to a stop at the house on Barnes Avenue, I found John safely at home! Those guys had turned that boat over on purpose, abandoned it there and swam to shore. They had taken another route back home.

John may never have known how much Hal and he had scared me that day long ago, that is, until he reads this article!

Practice water safety, folks, till I write again!

47

The Greenlee Boys and Their Stripped-down Model A

Daddy finally closed his shoe shop in 1952. And so ended *Five Generations of Shoe Repair*, as his sign had read. That must've seemed like the end of an era for those people who worked in the Post Office Arcade, too. Daddy had made life interesting for them, no doubt about it!

He brought all of his shoe repair machines home, and into our basement they went for storage. Daddy had shown some previous interest in working out of doors, and the time was ripe. So he became an employee of the Fuller Brush Company. He was a Fuller Brush Man. He did quite well at this job, and in 1953 we got our first new car, a Sand Piper Tan 6-cylinder Ford Customline! I swear, when I saw Daddy drive up in that beautiful machine, I couldn't have been happier if it were a Cadillac or a Mercedes!

He said that he was so used to the noisy old 1940 Ford that he traded in, that he drove from Heintzleman Ford in Orlando nearly to Eustis before he realized that he was still in second gear. He'd never driven a car that ran so smooth and quiet! I was not quite old enough for my driver's license, but I used to sit in that car and dream of driving it around.

Sometime in the early 1950s, Daddy took the Model A Ford that we still had and removed the body. All that was left from the windshield back was the steering wheel and the two front seats. He fashioned a wooden platform behind the seats, and it became a "sort of" truck. Although both of us knew how, only John was old enough to drive at that point. But I did drive it around on the vacant lot adjacent to our house.

For several years we had that funny-looking vehicle in many places in the local area. We even went as far as Deland once. I remember one time us trying to get home and we were "running on fumes!" But alas, we had only 6 cents between us. So we pulled into the Super Test station next to Pugh's Dry Cleaners on Bay Street. In those days an attendant would pump your gas for you. So we asked for 6 cents worth. He laughed heartily and gave us a little squirt of gas (probably more like 10 cents worth), and we made it to Barnes Avenue.

Two scary incidents come to my mind concerning that Model A. We were at the high school down behind the softball field where there were some high mounds of dirt. John gunned that old Ford and tried to climb one of those mounds. Failing to make it to the top, we were coasting back down the dirt pile backwards. Suddenly John let the clutch out and gunned it again! My seat could not take this sudden change of direction, and it tipped over backwards! Out I went and did a flip in the air, landing on my feet right behind the back bumper! Scared the fool outa me, but I was okay.

The other could have been worse. We were driving on Barnes Avenue before it was paved. Don't remember the circumstance, but somehow I fell off my seat and ended up partially under the Model A! John slammed on the brakes and I kept rolling until we stopped.

I would say that if there is a heaven for automobiles, that Model A is doing quite well today! And happily, so are John and I!

Good advice in those days: Remember to look both ways before you cross the street! The Greenlee boys might be coming!

48

The Ups and Downs of Chicken-Raisin'

Back in the 1940s and 50s, lots of folks in town had chickens. Mrs. Haines across Barnes Avenue from us had a large chicken yard and the Hammonds had both chickens and ducks. When I became a member of Future Farmers of America, I too had chickens. I was required to be doing a "project," something that had to do with things that future farmers would do.

The folks would buy me 20 biddies, those cute little yellow guys, and I would lovingly tend to them as they grew into young adulthood. The chicken pen was at first beside the garage and then a later pen was built behind it, where once the Eustis Junior Fire Department had been located. I've heard it said that people shouldn't let their children name their farm animals that will soon be taken to market. I needed that advice. I spent time with these "pets" of mine, and life was good in the chicken yard.

But sadly, my little chicks grew up. And the time would come when Daddy would say that we were going to have to start eating my friends. And most every Sunday after that announcement, the population of my chicken yard decreased. I sure hated to lose them, but folks, my grief was short-lived each week. Because Daddy was a master cook and his fried chicken ranks among the best I ever ate!

One of these biddies turned out to be a rooster. Now, we didn't eat him, but let him grow up and he turned into a beautiful specimen! He roamed our yard and he caught the eye of Mrs. Haines across the street. She offered me $3.00 for him, and I took it. He ended up in her chicken yard full of hens. I reckon he thought he'd died and gone to heaven.

Brother John and I learned how to hypnotize a chicken! Really. We would take one of them and lay it on the concrete floor of our garage. Holding its head upright and against the floor, we would draw a chalk line directly out from it's beak. The chicken would lie there, I reckon looking at that line, until we would touch it or make some noise. See? Not only is this article possibly entertaining, it is also educational! You got this vital bit of information and beat the high cost of education in the process!

I'll be "chicken" in with you again soon!

49

Dabbling in the Business World

There were a lot of neighborhoods in Eustis that from time to time in those late 40s-early 50s days, had Kool-Aid stands in operation by the local kids. I'm sure they still do. We would occasionally feel the wind of entrepreneurship blow through our very young souls. Seems it was usually Miriam and me setting up a stand on the side of Barnes Avenue. And before long, our monopoly of the business on our street would have to be shared by another stand probably 75 feet from ours. Janet and Earla Sue usually operated that one. And sometimes they were first with their stand and we became the competition.

Janet reminded me recently that once when I became a little too competitive by sabotaging their product with a handful of good ole Florida dirt, her big brother Dale showed me in a more physical way why I should not do that again. I did that? A cherub like me? (Even cherubs become fallen angels once in awhile!)

But folks, Barnes Avenue was not busy enough for two Kool-Aid stands! Heck, it wasn't busy enough for one! There was not much of a market for lukewarm Kool-Aid on that little-traveled clay road! Seems we would end up drinking most of our own product. And soon forgetting former business failures, we would repeat these ventures on a fairly regular basis. Don't know about you, but I cannot see a little Kool-Aid stand today without stopping and buying a large cup, gladly paying more than the going price! I love those smiles!

But we did enjoy a modicum of success in the selling of mistletoe during the Christmas holidays. We would climb most any tree in our neighborhood and pick those sprigs, and set up shop on Eustis Street near the Post Office Arcade entrance. Lots of folks would stop and buy from us young mistletoe merchants.

A couple of my friends, perhaps with a little more gumption than me, had paper routes. Once or twice I got up verrrrry early and rode my bicycle with Jerry Lloyd Davis on his route. It was a pretty long one, and twisted through most of the streets in our end of Eustis. It didn't take me long to realize that it was far too much work being done way too early to ever entice me to take a route!

Three of us guys decided that we would earn some money doing yard work of any kind. This "business" of ours lasted through one customer. A lady in a big house on Bay Street wanted us to not only clean up her yard, but also pull all the weeds, including their roots, in her garden. Folks, there were a zillion weeds in there and some had pretty tough root systems. Lord have mercy, we worked all day and thought we would die for sure before we finally finished that job. I don't think I've ever been that dirty since. For that magnificent effort, we each received a couple of bucks. Even in those early 1950s days, that was pitiful!

None of these things mentioned above would do much for my résumé. But it is how a lot of young guys and gals tried to make a little money back then.

50

Unscheduled Fireworks on Eustis Street

Part of the joy of growing up in Eustis was having a dad who was himself basically a kid, and him doing some of the things that I found very funny and would like to have done! I have mentioned some of his practical jokes in past articles. Well, here's one of my favorites.

At this time, Daddy's shoe shop was still located on Eustis Street near the Post Office Arcade entrance and next to Bennett's Grocery. Down the block on the other side of the Arcade entrance was Hoke Dollar's Fish Market. The setting is in the summertime, and in those days there just wasn't much business to be found, at least at Greenlee's Shoe Shop. (Idle hands are the devil's workshop...heh...heh.)

It was Daddy's custom to rush down to Hoke's Market and wash his hands between customers. But this time it was a special trip! Daddy told us that he rushed in as usual and Hoke was dozing in a chair. He didn't even stir when Daddy came in. In the back of the market, behind a curtain where the fish were cleaned, there was a sink where Daddy would wash his hands. A young fella who cleaned the fish was also snoozing back there. This time, instead of washing his hands, Daddy used the loud splattering of the water to cover the sound of the match he struck to light a string of fairly large firecrackers!

Rushing out, as usual, he made it just about back to his shop when the first firecracker went off! Daddy related that he regretted immediately that he had done it, because it sounded like World War II had come to Eustis

Street! Like cannons, those firecracker blasts brought Hoke and his fish-cleaner tearing out of the market! By this time, of course, Daddy was busy shining a pair of shoes or something.

Folks, that fish market had a real high ceiling and the concussion of the blasts brought down the old cracked plaster from up there! Not only that, but the fish-cleaning fella, in his panic, hit the wall so hard coming out from behind that curtain, that the plaster fell there, too! Word had it that the postmaster, Mr. Marley, had gotten down behind one of the post office windows with a six-shooter, and was prepared to defend the post office, if necessary!

Of course, Mr. Dollar highly suspected that Daddy had done this dastardly deed (lots of "d"s there, folks.), even though Daddy was acting as surprised as all of the other merchants on that block! So, in his way, the fish man soon got even with the cobbler. Hoke knew that Daddy was looking for some "stuffin'" to put in the dilapidated couch in his shop. Well, one day not long after, Hoke brought an old mattress up and placed it right on a pile of debris near the front of Daddy's shop. Exactly what Daddy had been looking for! Stuffin'!

He dragged that mattress into his place and cut it open. Soon he had handfuls of mattress innards! And soon also, Daddy began to itch on his arms. And then on his body. A close examination of that mattress revealed that it was highly infested with bedbugs! Daddy had to get his shoe shop fumigated! So I'd say that after that inning, the score was tied 1 – 1.

If you're beginning to itch, remember that it's just your imagination!

51

Leaving Skin on Hillcrest Drive

For Christmas probably in 1950 or 51, John and I got brand new Firestone bicycles! They were things of beauty! They included headlights and a horn. In fact, mine had everything I wanted on it… except brakes! Folks, you could do what you wanted to in trying to put on the brakes, and it was more like stepping on the clutch!

I told you about the brake situation because there is a tie-in in this incident. I was on my way to Lake Gracie with a couple of buddies. Now, one good way from Barnes Avenue to the lake is to go on Center Street to Lakeview Avenue. Take a right and go to Hillcrest Court. A left there will take you to Hillcrest Street that is on a steep hill, and it dead ends into Lake Gracie Drive at the bottom. Hillcrest in those days was tar and gravel in makeup.

At the top of the hill where Hillcrest Street starts, there lived a fearsome dog! We started down the hill and Mr. Dog chose me to be hostile to! Off to the races we went! He was nipping at my heels, and I was standing up, pumping those pedals on my Firestone as hard as my young legs could do it!

I was pleased at the considerable speed that I had mustered and that I had finally left that beast behind! But I was roaring down steep Hillcrest by then! In fact, I was going so fast that if I opened my mouth, my cheeks would pootch out from the wind! Now was the time to turn my attention back to things ahead. Friends, the bottom of that hill was upon me! Standing on my useless brakes, I studied very briefly the options I had: I could run straight across Lake Gracie Drive and smash into the large pine trees guarding that route. Or I could try to turn onto Lake Gracie Drive. Either way I figured I was as good as dead!

So I turned my wheel to the right as I neared the bottom! That bicycle immediately slid from under me, and I kid you not, the speed was so great that the wind picked it up like an airplane wing. It flew for a while. I didn't.

I landed on my right side and continued down that tar and gravel road! Folks, I was wearing a bathing suit. Period. The road commenced to sand away the hide from my ankle, my calf, my hip, my rib cage and my arm! When I finally stopped, I was a bleeding mess! A prudent person, no matter how young, would have decided to call it a day on the swimming, and head back home for some sympathy and first aid from his or her Mama. I went on swimming.

It realllly stung badly when I first went in the water! And it took a number of tries before I finally could stay in. And then guess what? It realllly stung badly to get out! So I spent over 3 hours in Lake Gracie, in less than sterile water! Oh mercy, did I pay for that!

Infection set in, in all of my contusions, and in spite of the best doctoring by Mama and a trip or two to Dr. Bowen, it took a long while for them to finally heal! I reckon if I had that one to do over again, I'd have just let the dog bite me!

The moral is this: A mean dog chasing an airhead on a brakeless bicycle down a tar and gravel road on a steep hill with extremely limited options at the bottom, often spells disaster! Don't let it happen to you!

And leash those dogs, folks!

52

Shower-Singing leads to State Competition

I'm thinking the following started when we were in the 10th grade, say 1952-53. After gym class, we guys would pile into the large shower room to get rid of a little sweat and dirt. There must have been about 6 shower heads in there. But the room had great acoustics! Some of us musically inclined boys began to sing while showering! James Moore, Jerry Lloyd Davis, Ronnie Butler and I, along with 3 or 4 more commenced to harmonize! And it really sounded pretty! I remember the first song we did: *String Along With Me.*

Coach Kelsey liked it so much that he had us come out of the shower and stand there with towels around us and sing for him. Then after we dressed, he marched us into the shop class going on next to the locker room. There we sang for that class!

From there we blossomed into singing for school assemblies. I think we were called the Locker Room Eight or something close to that. Out of this group, four of us became a quartet. We were James Moore, 1st tenor, Jerry Lloyd Davis, bass, Ronnie Butler, baritone and me as 2nd tenor or lead. We were invited to sing for the Kiwanis Club and then they sponsored us. They even bought us matching Panama suits (first suit I ever had) and we sang for them at each of their meetings.

That quartet went on to represent Eustis High School in the district and then the state quartet contest in Tampa. Our music teacher, whose name I forget, took us to the contest in her car. (I sure haven't forgotten what she looked like, and neither has any of the other guys!) I think we got honorable mention.

53

My Fateful Marble-Toss

Folks, something as harmless as a marble can actually cause a lot of trouble! It happened to me at Eustis High School along in probably 1951. I was most likely an eighth grader at the time. We were on the school grounds in front of EHS during lunch hour. Here's what happened.

Someone had thrown another fella's gym shorts up into the very large oak tree in front of the building, and we were trying to figure out how to get them down. Guys were tossing various things up there to try and dislodge them. I had a marble in my pocket. Big deal. You can't bring down a pair of gym shorts with a marble! But, what the heck.

Now, I was facing the school building as I threw my marble up into the tree. It missed the shorts, and somehow it missed every limb in that tree. But it didn't miss the upstairs window in one of the classrooms where class was in session! CLACK!

I went over and looked up at the window. From my vantage point it did not appear to be broken, and after a brief and fruitless search for my marble I went on to other things. But before long, a couple of policemen were coming up the front sidewalk. They seemed to be on a mission of some sort, and I wondered about that a little.

And when we went back to classes after lunch break we were met with the news that a bullet had been fired from somewhere and had crashed through an upstairs classroom window during the lunch hour. The police were sweeping the floor of that classroom looking for the bullet. We were also informed that patrol cars had been sent all across Eustis, looking for someone with a rifle who might have carelessly fired it in the direction of the school.

The window in that classroom did have a neat little hole in it that looked indeed like a bullet had come through. But I, and only I, knew better! Searching continued both in and outside the building for the bullet I knew they would never find. Police were still scouring the neighborhoods looking for a shooter I knew did not exist. Lord, I didn't mean to cause all this trouble, and now should I step forward and tell them that I was responsible for the hole in the window? Or should I just keep my trap shut?

I decided to confess, but not to the school officials. I told my mama. Bless her heart, she immediately called the school and told the principal the story of my errant marble toss. Well, he called off the bullet and shooter search right away. The principal was not upset that I had accidentally hit the window; but he was a little perturbed with me for not telling him or someone right away that I had done it.

I maintained my fairly good standing as a junior-higher and didn't even have to pay for the window. Let me close this with a little marble talk. How many of you remember this statement and what it meant: "Kiss and ties first, last lagger!"

Hold on to your marbles as long as you can, folks.

54

The Day my Sin was "Erased"

Have you ever thrown something that you wished you hadn't? In my last article it was a marble. Well, Lord have mercy, it happened to me again one day at Eustis High School! I'm guessing I was a freshman, so that was probably in 1951 or early 52. One of my friends and I were in the habit of ambushing each other as we entered the classroom. Chalkboard erasers were good for that! They rarely caused permanent injury and a direct hit on the "enemy" would produce a cloud of white chalk powder! Such ambushes could turn into some real battles before the teacher would come in.

Aha! I was going to be first into the room that day! I was ahead of my friend, and I grabbed 3 or 4 erasers and stood in the back of the room, throwing arm cocked into position, eraser ready to fly! "Just step through that door, buddy boy, and you're dead meat!," I muttered to myself. But right here's where this "surprise attack" began to turn sour. Unbeknownst to me, my friend stopped at his locker. *He wasn't supposed to do that*! Because that meant that he would not be the next one to enter the door!

On that fateful day our wonderful teacher, Mrs. Ruth Rice, had to be out and a rather gruff, stoutly built man was the substitute. Well, footsteps were approaching the classroom door, and my trigger was ready to be squeezed. My timing was perfect even if my judgment wasn't! Because by the time that eraser was passing my ear and leaving my hand, I knew that I was the dead meat! Thank the Lord my aim was off just a centimeter or two. That eraser zzzzzipped past the nose of that substitute teacher, not missing him by more than a couple of inches!

Now folks, there is a certain amount of honor among mischievous boys and had there been any one of them at all in that room with me, perhaps we could have finger-pointed at each other or something, but no. It was just the substitute and me. His head slowly turned to look at me, and I'll bet I looked like a deer caught in the headlights! This culminated in my immediate departure for the office of the assistant principal, Mr. Chester Crowder, where I was the recipient of some of his corrective guidance. Ahh, that office; I knew it well…for all the wrong reasons!

Please be good.

55

From their Mouths to God's Ear

Daddy and Mama moved from Winter Haven to Eustis in 1935, and Daddy opened his shoe repair shop on Eustis Street downtown. But Mama never lost her close attachment to her family and her hometown of Bartow. That is the reason that not one of us three children was born at Waterman Memorial.

John was born in 1936, I in 1937 and Miriam in 1939. Each of these births was preceded by a three hour, 90-mile trip to Bartow made by a very pregnant mother-to-be, bumping along in a Model T Ford. But this strong bond with her home that Mama had, gave us some very happy times in those early years. Literally, each month would find us clattering along in our Model T and then our later car, a 1929 Model A Ford, on the way to Bartow to spend seven days with "Gonga" and Grandpa. ("Gonga" was named by brother John and is a variation of the word "Grandma".)

I have told you this to set the stage for a memory of childhood that this Eustis boy had in Bartow. It took place in the dark days of World War II, on the main street of that little central Florida town. I was walking with Gonga when the fire station whistle blew. The precise time was 11:59 a.m.

Upon that whistle sounding, everybody all over town stopped what they were doing immediately! On the sidewalk, in the grocery store, in their cars, or wherever or whatever, heads were bowed in prayer to the Almighty about the war. Promptly at noon the whistle sounded again and people resumed their activities.

Perhaps that same scenario was taking place in other cities across the nation, but Bartow was the only one I knew about. That made a lasting impression on this little boy. As best I can remember, there was no outcry against the practice and no court demanding a cessation of public prayer to God. It was a time of people in trouble calling out to their God who answered their prayers.

He's still the same God.

56

The Poorly-Thrown Butcher Knife

You will notice that in several of my articles I make confessions. It is good for the soul, sez the Bible, and besides, after 50 - 60 years or so, who's going to punish me?

Aunt Mary and Cousins Annette and Bobby were visiting us from Bartow. And I was just trying to perfect the skill of throwing a butcher knife and making it stick in the camphor berry tree trunk in the front yard. Two seemingly unrelated sentences, huh? As a 14 year old in early 1952 I might have wished that they had remained unrelated.

Our house on Barnes Avenue did not have a paved driveway in those days, so family and visitors all pulled into the yard in various locations to park. One great shady spot to park was near the camphor berry tree. So Aunt Mary had pulled her brand spankin' new 1952 Ford Mainline into that place. It was a beauty, and at that time neither we nor our kinfolks drove many new cars. So we all had looked it over and admired it earlier in the day.

Well folks, it was time for me to throw my butcher knife again. And at my usual target. Never mind that Aunt Mary's beautiful new machine was only slightly off center of the flight of my knife and just to the left of the tree. You think that mattered to me? Didn't even cross my mind!

The butcher knife zipped through the air and stuck in the tree trunk! Boy, was I getting good at it! The next speeding knife was not quite as well thrown... It glanced off that tree trunk and in a flash had smacked Aunt Mary's new car right at the top of the back fender! If I'd had a pacemaker it would have kicked in right then! Wide-eyed I looked around and nobody had seen this incident!

I walked haltingly to the car and looked at the fender. Sure enough, there was about a 3-inch line dent made by the blade whacking it. It wasn't deep enough so that it jumped right out at you and one would probably have to be looking for it to see it. But to me it looked like the Grand Canyon!

I made a choice at this point. I could either go and confess and throw myself on Aunt Mary's mercy, or I could just say nothing and see if anyone noticed. I chose silence and I reckon no one noticed it. Aunt Mary lived out in the country near Bartow and she finally parked that car in her front yard. And it sat in that same spot after its useful life, until it rusted out many years later. Once, after I was a grownup, I walked up to that old car and looked carefully for the famous dent. I could not find it.

Now I feel better! Thanks for reading my confession! Kids, check with your mom before throwing a butcher knife at anything! I shoulda.

57

My Miracle Catch

As I said in an earlier episode, baseball was my life in the early 50s! I'm sure that the other sports had their good points, but none of them appealed to me like baseball! I am not a terribly gifted athlete and I probably worked a little harder than some of the others to produce acceptable results.

I was rather proud that my batting average was pretty good in high school. But every young struggling player needs something special to happen to him or her at least once. It happened for me during a high school baseball game in Apopka. I was playing left field and was no doubt playing too shallow.

One of those Apopka sluggers smacked a line drive that was obviously going to be over my head and would roll all the way to the fence! The guy would probably have an inside-the-park homerun!

Well, I tore out toward the fence, fully intending to retrieve the ball and accept the humiliation of not playing my field correctly. But I ran as fast as my legs would allow, and when I thought the ball might just be passing overhead somewhere at that moment, I leapt as high as I could with my glove turned around backward!

And SMACK! Somehow and the Lord only knows how, that baseball slammed itself right into the pocket of my glove! (I had no idea I was within 15 feet of it!) I had made a brilliant catch! Even the Apopka fans were applauding me! It was the third out and I then had the privilege of trotting in to this continuing round of appreciation of what I had done!

Folks, the Lord has a way of keeping me from being too proud of myself! As I came in smiling and waving to the fans, I bumped my head on the dugout roof! Near about knocked myself out! I'm not sure, but I hope that clumsy act on my part was not witnessed by too many of those fans.

But a couple of innings later, the hero became just the regular struggling outfielder he really was. There was a short fly ball to center field that that fielder would not be able to get to. I ran over, took a dive at it and as I rolled on the ground it looked like I had caught it! Two great catches in one game? No.

Alas, when I hit the ground the ball dislodged from my glove. In fact, I never really had it securely in my glove. The glory was now just a memory! Coach Bill Kelsey told me later that he was glad that I dropped it. He said that they would not have been able to live with me afterward if I had caught that one, too! Coach may have had a point!

Batter up!

58

When I Became an Unwelcome
Guest at a Church Picnic

Although Eustis had a number of fine places to swim, it was always a special treat to go to Rock Springs. Located between Sorrento and Apopka, the Springs was close enough to get there in just a little while. If you've been there, you know that the water flows from two large holes in a gigantic rock. Icy and crystal clear, it makes it's way into a rather large swimming area, and then it flows on downstream to what is called the first landing and then farther on to the second landing.

Although one could walk a path to those landings on down the river, it was much more fun to go by water. Actually a normal size guy would find the water not over his head except in a couple of places going to the first landing. I never made it to the second one.

Of the memorable occasions at Rock Springs, one sticks out in my mind. And it was not a very pleasant one. I had been invited by a friend to go on a picnic sponsored by his church. And we were having a great time, horsing around as guys do. Let me add to this story that the hamburgers were being cooked under a shed with a tin roof. And through the years of cooking under it, a great coating of soot had built up under the roof right over the grille.

I reckon I was showing off a little by demonstrating to the other guys how high I could throw one of the large nuts that grew on those trees there. I did get one of them up a pretty good ways. The "going up" was beautiful, but the descent was terrifying for me and the landing was tragic! I say terrifying because I could see where it was going to come crashing down!

My missile did not come straight back down as I had planned. No, it veered slightly off course and came down with a monstrous "KA-BAM" right on that tin roof! This was followed by immediate cries of dismay from under the shed! Alas, much of that accumulated soot suddenly became unattached and whumped down right on those half-done hamburgers!

Folks, I have never seen so many fingers pointing at me in my life! And let's just say that I was not the most popular individual at the picnic! It ruined most of the hamburgers! I felt terrible about it and even worse because I was a visitor, an invited guest. You know, now that I think about it, I don't believe that I ever was asked to go with them again!

There'll be more.

59

The Hit that changed it all

As time passed by and we boys got a little older in the early 1950s, the side yard baseball field on Barnes Avenue became much too small. Heck, it was too small to begin with, but we managed until we found a place for a new one!

The Butlers lived at the corner of Grove Street and Lakeview Avenue. It seems that they owned the whole block stretching down to Eustis Street, but except for their house on that corner, it was undeveloped. So gathering up all of our nerve, several of us knocked on their door. They were most gracious and said it would be fine for us to build a baseball field there. (Of course that was in the days when insurance matters and lawsuits were unheard of when it came to the liability issues. Back then if we were to get hurt on that field, we would just get over it. And we did, and we did!)

We had more fun cutting the high weeds down and fashioning a very large baseball field! And that field got some real good use for several years. Those times were before Little League Baseball came along. But we fellas were just as happy without it.

We did have American Legion Baseball, however, and several of us played on that team. We would go as far away as Belleview and Wildwood to play. Though I was never good enough to pitch on the high school team, I did pitch with some success on the Legion team. Mostly though, I was an outfielder. Like I said before, if love and desire were all that it took to be a great baseball player I would have been a "shoo in" for the major leagues!

I did play on the Eustis Panthers baseball team from 1953 to 1955. Most of the time I started, but I think it was because we didn't have many on our roster. I started out batting 9th, and I remember the coach telling me to "get a walk" and "don't swing at the ball." I was kinda small in stature and my strike zone was not real big. But I wanted to hit!

A defining moment came for me and my self-confidence at the Eustis Ball Park one afternoon. I disobeyed the coach's orders. There were runners on 1st and 2nd base and we were behind by a run. I received my "don't swing/ get a walk" speech as I went to bat. The first pitch whizzed right in there belt-high and was a strike! I knew I could have hit it!

I decided if another came like that, I was going to take a cut at it. It did...and I did. The cry "NOOOOOO..." from the coach was drowned out by the unmistakable sound of a baseball meeting a fiercely-swung bat! It was a line drive hit over the leftfielder's head! And those two runners scored as I stood proudly on 2nd base with a double! We won that game.

The coach had a few words to say to me afterward about obeying his voice, but never again was I instructed to wait for a walk and not to swing. (I batted over .300 that year. Not too shabby, I reckon.)

Remember to tag up on a fly ball now.

60

When "Lucky" Went to Heaven

Mama was quite involved in the First Baptist Church throughout our growing up years, and in fact remained active in church work until her death at age 92. She used to attend what they called Circle Meetings (not sure why the name). Our church sponsored several "Circles" that were named for saintly women of the church. I remember one was called the Tidie Formby Circle. I happen to remember Tidie and her husband Clark. And fine Christian people they were.

I recall one winter in the mid-1940s when Tidie and Clark showed up at our front door. They brought with them a brand new blanket and gave it to Mama. Surprised by this, Mama asked what it was for. And the Formbys told her it was a gift to her because she was the best Christian they knew. They were right in their assessment of Mama, at least to this little boy. She was the best Christian that I knew too. But I think another reason for the blanket gift was that they thought we needed it.

Well, as I recall, Mama was a member of the Tidie Formby Circle, and one particular Circle Meeting night, the women met at Mrs. Hale's house out Orange Avenue. Now Mrs. Hale had a parakeet that was quite the bird! He was friendly and could talk up a storm. I was told that among other things, he could say, "Hello, my name is Lucky Hale, and I live on Orange Avenue in Eustis."

He was the hit of the evening for awhile as he flitted around that living room full of ladies who were sitting pretty much in a circle (Hey, maybe that was why they were called Circles!). After a bit the program for the evening got started and they began talking about supporting missionaries and other ministry-related subjects. Lucky Hale was forgotten.

Mama said that the better part of an hour had passed when Mrs. Hale noticed that Lucky wasn't somewhere in the room with them. But they went on with their meeting. Little did any of them realize that Lucky Hale had not left the room, but that his "luck" had most recently run out. I reckon I should add at this point that several of those ladies were quite well padded and this fact might have added to Lucky's plight.

When the meeting adjourned and the ladies all got up from their soft seats on the couch and in easy chairs, poor Lucky was found quite lifeless underneath one of those ladies. Evidently she had leaned forward and he had flown down behind her, and "whammo!" He probably didn't know what hit him! And perhaps due to her padding she could not detect that little struggling lump under her.

Not sure if the Formby Circle ever met there again. So remember to cage your bird before the missionary group meets in your living room.

61

The Day my Kick made a Real Change to the Scoreboard

Yeh, we weren't supposed to be in there. Let's say the year was 1951, and the old gymnasium on the corner of Bay Street and Woodward Avenue was off limits to everybody except when being used for sporting events. That being said, it was very easy to circumvent the locked doors in that ancient structure and many a youngster had been inside clandestinely.

Likewise, a group of us had gone in to play a little basketball. I reckon that in itself would have been harmless enough. However, one of us had brought a football in there with him this time. Soon our attention turned to trying a new game with the football. We would try to place-kick the football the length of the basketball court in the slightest of chances that it might go through the basketball goal net.

Important to this episode is a rather attractive scoreboard hanging high on the wall at the far end of the gym. I remember during basketball games that as the hands counted down the minutes, the face of the clock would change colors. That scoreboard was probably the nicest thing in the old place.

Well, there we were with one of us holding the football at one end of the floor and each taking a turn place-kicking it toward the other end. Most of the kicks were going pretty much in the direction of the goal down there, although no one had put it through the net. Well, folks, it was my turn.

Football was not my sport and I was rather proud as my kick sent the ball soaring quite long and high! And…it was going straight at it…it looked like it would be a direct hit! And it was! Only it wasn't the basketball net at the other end. It was that scoreboard clock, folks. My kick was at a 45 degree angle to the goal! I could have kicked footballs the remainder of that afternoon and all the next day and not come near that clock!

We all watched in transfixed horror as that football slammed into the face of the clock with a sickening KABLAMPF! And the beautiful plastic face was now broken. Badly broken! I had made the bad kick and it had been witnessed by 4 or 5 other boys.

Well, it didn't take long to clear out of that place! This confession of my guilt is the first time its been made known in these 55 years. But I was terrified all the next basketball season that one of my friends, if put under pressure, might divulge my secret. At the games I do not recall much ever being said about the broken clock face, and shortly thereafter they tore the old gymnasium down.

If this confession on my part causes me trouble after all these years, I will fight extradition to Florida.

62

Car Receives "Miracle Cure"

I like to relate some of the shenanigans my dad was involved in during my growing up years. This one ranks right up there among the best. I have mentioned previously that Dad had a friend who had the fish market down Eustis Street from his shoe shop. Hoke Dollar and Herb Greenlee were a dangerous duo!

In this incident, a fella who worked for a local furniture company had parked his car in front of Daddy's shoe shop on Eustis Street while he went into Bennett's Grocery next door. Opportunity knocked and Hoke and Daddy answered the door! While this unwitting gent was grocery shopping, they took his jack from his car and jacked the rear end up just enough so that the drive wheel would not touch the street. Innocent little prank it was, but it was about to spin into something far better, at least for the pranksters!

This fella came back and got into his car, started it and put it in reverse. Nuthin! He put it in a forward gear. Nuthin! Now, instead of taking a minute to walk around the car where he would have easily spotted the trouble, he simply walked back to his place of employment which was down Magnolia Avenue to where it intersects with Bay Street. Dad and Hoke took this opportunity to put the jack back in the car. After a while this gent and his boss came driving up in the boss's car. Together, while Daddy was "busy fixing some shoes" and Hoke was "tied up selling some fish", those two men pushed that car out into the middle of Eustis Street and hooked a chain on the front.

His boss then pulled the car to the corner and down Orange Avenue toward Bay Street. Now the rest of this tale comes from Daddy's later talk with that boss. He had actually pulled this perfectly good car about 7 miles to the employee's house over toward Umatilla.

He told Daddy that after they had finally gotten home with the car and had unhooked the chain, the man had said to him, "Now watch this. I'll show you what I mean about the car not working." Then starting the car, he put it in gear and let out the clutch. The automobile had lurched forward almost running over his boss!

Although Daddy and Hoke were in a near state of collapse at this news, I don't think either one of them ever told the recipient of their prank or his boss the reason for the temporary mechanical failure of the automobile on that day!

Life with Daddy was often a hoot, folks.

63

High Drama on the Highway

Recently I was in a local shoe repair shop, and the fragrance in the air took me back to fond memories. As you know, Daddy operated a shoe repair shop. There is a certain aroma found in a shoe shop – that of leather perhaps mixed with various glues and polishes. It hasn't changed throughout the long years.

Every so often Daddy would have to go to Orlando to purchase a "bin" of leather. A bin is a very large piece of leather that Daddy would convert into half and full soles. He would first trace out his pattern and then with a special leather knife he would cut them out as near to the correct size as possible to conserve his supply of leather.

The trip to Orlando was often a family occasion. Daddy would drive the Model A Ford down Hwy 441 to "The City Beautiful" until Church Street intersected. We would come near to the center of the city and then turn down a side street and stop at Tetenbaum's Leather Supplies. After Daddy's purchase had been made it was fun time! We would often go to Kress' Five and Ten Cent Store. That well-stocked Dime Store was more like the Magic Kingdom for me. And we kids usually came away from there with a few carefully chosen trinkets.

With the day nearly spent we would head back up Church Street. I remember that the street lights would be on by that time and they were amber in color, which Daddy liked a lot! I think the color reminded him of autumn, his favorite season. He would comment on them each time.

I recall a sense of well-being as we rode along, John, Miriam and I sharing the back seat with that bin of leather. I believe that it had to do with my knowledge that Daddy now had enough material to do his shoe repairing for some weeks. For some reason those kinds of worries were a part of my young make-up.

A harrowing experience happened one time as we had turned onto Orange Blossom Trail heading for Eustis. Our Model A had notoriously bad brakes, but Daddy had learned to control the car in spite of them. But this time as we rounded a curve we were suddenly upon a gaggle of cars just sitting still. They were parked in odd directions and I reckon there was an accident in the middle there somewhere. Well, Daddy couldn't stop… and God took over!

Daddy twisted and turned that car through that maze and somehow, and only the Lord knows how, we didn't hit any person or any other car. I really cannot remember any yelling or conversation at all as we went through that mess! We were all too scared! Well, Daddy was sure that the police would come after us, but they must've been too busy with whatever was going on there. Our Guardian Angel hopefully received some sort of merit badge for his help this time!

64

Showin' 'em My Stuff

In a previous article I told you that I was not much of a diver. I just did not have the fluid moves to make it anything special. But I will share with you one of my most embarrassing moments as a young teen and it had to do with a dive.

The scene of my embarrassment was the new swimming pool behind the McClelland Band Shell in Ferran Park. I had gotten so that I could do a simple flip from the board in an acceptable fashion. But I longed to do a little more than that. Bill Andrews and some of the guys were steadily doing these fancy dives and doing them well.

So I had finally gotten the nerve to move on from the simple flip to a flip and a half! Friend Bill was my teacher. And after some work on it, which included sometimes drinking portions of the pool's contents, I got so I could do a pretty good "one-and-a-half-er."

Now was the time to show off my new skill. To set the scene here, let me remind you that I was a very timid little guy when girls were involved. I liked them a lot, but was scared to get too close to them! There were several girls at the pool that afternoon that I considered to be pretty neat! Could it be that I could impress them a little?

I asked them to come to the deep end and watch me do my "one-and-a-half-er." To my delight they were happy to come and watch me! And so, as they fixed their eyes on me, I climbed the ladder to the diving board. "Okay, big boy, show 'em your stuff!" Little did I know that this was a prophetic utterance!

With a smooth start I began to accelerate toward the end of the board, and springing once and landing on the board's business end I was soon hurtling through space! Things were going well! I grabbed my knees and went into the flip. At the right moment I released my knees, opened up into a reasonably straight head down body position and hit the water arms extended and I knew I had nailed a good one! So far so good!

Folks, here's where it went bad. I had not tied the string inside my bathing suit. I did not usually tie it, but this time I shoulda. As the water rushed past my face and received the rest of my body, the extreme force of it grabbed my bathing suit and pulled it right off of me! It zoomed all the way down to my ankles and the jockey got caught on my foot, or I'da been swimming around down there looking for it!

The water was very clear and I knew I now had no anatomical secrets from those two girls up there! I had definitely "showed 'em my stuff"…all of it! I hastily pulled the suit back on while near the bottom of the deep end. Then I swam underwater as far as I could until I had to come up to breathe, heading for the shallow end.

Out of the pool I got and I went home. I do not recall either the girls or me ever mentioning that incident to each other. But I bet they had a hay day telling their friends about it!

Boys, that string is in there for a good reason! Use it!

65

Discovering a New Entrance to the Bedroom

Two of my childhood friends, brothers, lived a block from me. This episode happened probably in 1953. So I was 15 years old and the two friends a year and two years younger. To set the stage, that family had inherited an almost new Kaiser car. It was a blue beauty with all of the whistles and bells on it.

Because the family already had a very nice Oldsmobile 98, that Kaiser spent a lot of time just sitting in the garage. Both parents worked downtown, and they used the Olds to get to and from there. Folks, young teen boys will not just let a fine auto like that Kaiser sit in the garage forever! Oh, we should have.

The older of those boys, upon close examination of the car, discovered that when the ignition switch was in a certain position, the key could be removed and the starter would still engage when the switch was turned. Our sitting in it and starting it up soon became passé, and we began to feel the need for a ride in that vehicle.

So, with his brother and a couple of us ensconced in those nice seats, my buddy backed carefully from the garage onto Grove Street. And quickly we were clipping down toward the Old Mount Dora Road. The fact that our driver had never driven before was no deterrent at all! He managed to keep it on the right side of the road, and with horn tooting at most anything we passed, we had a ball!

So far so good! Now it was time to go home. So, turning around at the Old Mount Dora Road intersection, we zoomed up Grove Street again, and turned into his driveway. The car slowed as it should when we prepared to enter the garage! In just a few moments we would be out of that car, with his parents being none the wiser.

Let me add here, folks, that the bedroom of those two brothers was connected to the back of the garage by a common wall. This is important, because we were about to discover a new way to enter that bedroom! Right! As our driver moved his foot to the brake pedal (he thought), the car suddenly lurched forward and smashed it's nose right into that bedroom! He had pressed the accelerator instead of the brake!

I mean there were broken two-by-fours, wallboard and all! The grille and front end of that beautiful car were a mess! Fluid poured out of the radiator and pooled under it! Four terrified boys stood looking at that scene, each wishing we were far from it! What now?

Here was the decision by my friend. He would say nothing about it. And in that his parents carried the keys, they might just blame each other for the accident! Folks, unbelievable, but that's exactly what happened! He never got blamed at all for it, but his parents had a number of heated discussions between themselves about it. The car was soon fixed, and the wall of the bedroom repaired, but the "mystery accident" remained unsolved.

Years passed, and after we were adults my friend and I talked on one of my visits to Eustis. I asked him when it was that he finally admitted to his parents that he had wrecked the car and house. He said he had never told them! So you will notice that I did not use his name, thereby protecting the guilty!

66

The Bogus Soft Drink

I like to mix some antics of my dad's in amongst these vignettes of my childhood. Here is a good one. On a fairly regular basis, Daddy would meet with Hoke Dollar of the fish market and Mr. Bennett at Bennett's Grocery Store, next to Daddy's Shoe Shop on Eustis Street in the mid-1940s. I reckon they were the "Three Musketeers of Eustis." These three buddies would gather when business was down, and they had a real good relationship going. I say that, knowing that Mr. Bennett had a bit of a problem with Daddy for awhile after one of their bull sessions.

Upon meeting they would get soft drinks from the cooler. Well, Daddy couldn't help but notice the peculiar way that Mr. Bennett drank his Coca Cola. He would open it, turn it up and gulp down half of it, take a breath, and gulp down the other half! Remember now, these were those little bottles back then. Well, Daddy's mind got to working overtime about how he could use Bennett's manner of gulping his drinks in a prank. And he came up with a good one!

He snuck an empty Coke bottle and a cap from Bennett's store, and washed them carefully. Into the bottle he poured Postum! (Postum is a breakfast drink still sold today.) And he pushed the cap onto the bottle that now looked like the real McCoy, just like Coca Cola for sure. See this one coming?

Going into Bennett's Grocery, he went to the drink cooler and placed that bottle way back in the corner so nobody else would get it! (That woulda probably been even funnier!) Well, the time finally came for the 3 guys to get together as usual. And Daddy, being extra magnanimous that day, offered to buy drinks for the other two. "Make mine a Coke," said the unsuspecting Bennett. Daddy reached far back in the cooler and got his "special Coke" for Bennett. He popped the caps off and casually handed the guys their drinks of choice.

Trying not to notice, Daddy could see Bennett taking that beautiful cold drink of Postum toward his mouth. And…there it went! Bennett had it turned upside down, gulping it down to the halfway point! So far so good. But as Bennett lowered the bottle and took a breath, all heck broke loose! He let out a loud gag, slapped his hand over his mouth, and ran out the front door of his store and on to the sidewalk! Out there, if he didn't lose everything he had eaten in the past two days, he missed a good chance!

Now, Daddy would have had a hard time passing the blame for that one to someone else, because he handed Bennett the drink. And as was often the case, the victim in Daddy's pranks was not amused. But it wasn't long until Bennett, Dollar and Greenlee were back at their old ways of enjoying each other's company. I have an idea, though, that there was never a Coke that Bennett drank after that, that he didn't think of this dastardly act by my dad.

So, next time you and I get together, I'll flip ya for a Postum!

67

Daddy the Halloween Ghost

Halloween was my favorite celebration as a kid. Not only the "trick or treat" part of it, but what took place at our house on Barnes Avenue. In the early days of our living there, say the mid to late 40s, we had an old wooden garage behind the house. On one side there was a trellis that went the length of the garage for various vines to grow on. And behind that trellis was enough space to walk comfortably.

Daddy fashioned a "spook house" of sorts behind the trellis for the neighborhood children to come and walk through. He was good at doing those things, and much fun was had by all! At other Halloween events, he would fix our cellar (yes, we had one…) with the "spook house" scenario. I can still hear the squeals and screams of the kids as they experienced what he cooked up in those things!

After the spook house fun, Daddy would cook hamburgers on his camp stove for all of us! Then we would take to the neighborhood for treats or tricks. But I reckon the one having the most fun in all of this was Daddy. He loved the fall of the year, the harvest season, and the temperature changes that October brought. So Halloween gave him the perfect occasion to celebrate what he loved best! And it made our house a most popular place in the neighborhood!

Another thing that Daddy liked to do at Halloween was to get into a long white cylinder of cloth to look like a ghost! Don't know where he got that thing, but it covered his whole considerable body. He also had a horrible witch face that he would put on to top it off. I remember cooking it up with him ahead of time. At other times my brother John would be the

130

accomplice. It would be at night, and often we had friends and even small cousins at the house. Daddy would put that "get up" on in the bedroom. And at an agreed time his helper would go the back porch and reach in the meter box and cut the juice off to the whole house.

Pitch blackness brought exclamations of startled wonder from the kids. Then at the count of 10, John or I would turn the electricity back on, and Daddy would be standing in the room in the midst of all of them! Shrieks and flying feet resulted immediately! I remember that Mama thought that he shouldn't tease us so, but it was all part of who Daddy was and that was the way we loved him!

I know I share quite a bit about the kind of man my dad was, but he brought a lot of sunshine to those who knew him. I miss him.

68

Homemade Canoes

One of my early articles has to do with Lake Gracie, and the great times I had there with friends back in the 1940s and 50s. That particular article sparked some letters, email and "snail mail", as others shared memories in which that lake had a part. I gladly share some of these memories now.

Bob Andrews told me some time ago about his brother H. V. building a corrugated tin canoe as did his friend, Dick Giles. And about the good times they had tooling around Lake Gracie in them. Well, I thought that to be pretty interesting, and then I heard from his sister, Alice (Andrews) Harden, who went into some detail about these canoes. I want to both quote and paraphrase her letter to me.

Alice said that the boys took pieces of corrugated tin about 12 feet long and bent them in the middle lengthwise. They attached either end to a 1 x 2 board with nails and melted tar. They then flattened the bottoms slightly so they wouldn't tip over too easily. They sported a board seat near the middle. Alice said that made it easier to paddle and also more comfortable in case of leaks! Brother Bob reminded her that H. V. and Dick had split garden hoses lengthwise and fitted them over the raw edges to keep from getting cut.

Alice even sent me a picture of Dick and H. V. holding their canoes up while standing in the shallow water of Lake Gracie. The photo was taken in the early 1930s. She said that as the boys' interest turned toward building kayaks (which they did), she "inherited" these two canoes.

Now I want to quote Alice's letter in part: "Speaking of leaks – one afternoon our cousin, Jerald Drawdy of Mount Dora, and I were on Lake Gracie in the canoes, just having fun. We had been across the lake lengthwise, from south to north and were on our way back about halfway when I heard my cousin call out, "Help, Allie, I'm sinking!" And he was. I turned to look and Jerald and canoe were going down fast. He just held his hands up in the air and went down with the canoe. When he returned to the surface, he caught hold of the end of my canoe and I towed him in to land.

Luckily, our Mom had a nice sense of humor and didn't worry too much about us in the water as we spent half our time (there) in the summertime. She just laughed and said that should teach us not to depend on my brother's handiwork!"

It occurs to me that that tin canoe is probably still lying on the floor of Lake Gracie. Imagine someone in a future generation finding it and exclaiming on the technology of our era based on it. Thank you, Bob and Alice, for sharing.

69

The Log Cabin Playhouse

When we moved from Belmont Heights onto Barnes Avenue in Eustis in 1943, the lot beside our house on the left was vacant. There were portions of a foundation remaining after many years at the rear of it. We were told that once there was a garage apartment there.

Well, in that our yard was quite small, the folks scraped together what finances they could, and they purchased that lot! Many happy memories took place on it, including softball and camping out with friends in tents! But I want to relate something that we Greenlee kids had that most others did not.

Daddy built us a log cabin at the back of the lot. I mean it looked authentic! He got permission from some sawmill and went to collect their scrap pieces of lumber that still had pine bark on them. They were flat on one side and were perfect for his construction idea!

I suppose the building was 7 feet by 10 feet or so. It was complete with windows and a door made of the same stuff. Daddy even put a loft in it. John, Miriam, I and many of our neighborhood friends had much fun playing in that thing throughout our young childhood.

But even cleverly designed objects sometimes fall into misuse and disrepair after a time. So it was with this fine playhouse. I don't remember whose idea it was (Perhaps John's or friends David or Dale's), but it was finally agreed to by us guys that the cabin should be buried. That is, we could sink it into the ground, and hollow the inside dirt out and form a nifty bunker-type clubhouse! Marvelous idea!

The digging did not get very far, however. Not more than a foot or two down we ran into a solid sheet of concrete! As we cleaned away the dirt, we realized we had discovered the septic tank from that ancient garage apartment that had stood on that site. With much excitement and great difficulty, we finally managed to pry the lid up from it. Shoot, folks, it had been literally decades since its last use!

Guess what? There was absolutely nothing inside that thing! Absolutely nothing! It was like brand new! I thought it would be great to utilize it for that underground clubhouse we were trying to make with the cabin! After all, it was a right good size! (Well, at least big enough for very small club meetings.)

Mama pitched a royal fit when she heard these intentions! The septic tank was soon filled with dirt and the log cabin was finally torn down. And so, to this day, my record is clean with it comes to ever having played in a septic tank, thanks to Mama!

70

Close Call at Alexander Springs

I nearly caused a friend to drown in my early teens. It was probably in 1949 or 50, and I would have been in the sixth or seventh grade. This would be the day that I learned a lesson I have never forgotten!

I was a member of what we called Royal Ambassadors, a boys group, at the First Baptist Church. And we had taken an outing up into the Ocala National Forest or The Scrub as it was known, and were picnicking at Alexander Springs. In those days Alexander Springs was a beautiful place, with a long dock going out to where the huge spring was boiling up from deep in the ground. The water was ice cold and crystal clear!

And we boys were having a great time, whoopin' it up and jumping or diving into that spring! That was all of us except Jimmy. Jimmy was wearing his bathing suit, but had stopped about halfway out that long dock and was watching a man fish. We had asked him to come on out and join us a number of times, and he each time said he would be out soon.

Well, folks, soon never came. So I decided that I would take it upon myself to see that Jimmy did swim that day! And here's what I did. I walked back to where he was and stood there as if I too were interested in this guy fishing. Then suddenly and without warning, I shoved Jimmy off that dock into a very deep hole!

Down Jimmy went, thrashing around and all, and when he came to the surface the look of sheer terror on his face told me everything I wished I had known before! He screamed, "HELP...I CAN'T SWIM!" And down he went again! Now folks, I could swim enough at that time to get myself out of the water, but pulling somebody else out was beyond my capability!

Here's where the Good Lord was watching over his kids! The next time Jimmy broke water, that fisherman simply put his fishing pole right into Jimmy's hand! He latched on to it with white knuckles as he was pulled over to the dock and we helped him back up on it.

Jimmy was full of tears and I was full of apologies. We soon shook hands and all returned to normal. I think Jimmy and I both learned a lesson that day: I learned to never push someone into the water without knowing if he can swim, and Jimmy learned to either find out how to swim or to be sure to tell all others that he could not!

71

Eustis On The Air

In the mid-1940s, radio station **WEUS** came into being, and was housed in the rather impressive-looking white stucco building with white columns on Magnolia Avenue that was once the Eustis Chamber of Commerce. It was quite a novelty for Eustis to have its own station!

After some time, **WEUS** either went out of business or was bought by a new owner and the call letters became **WLBE**. One program that had wide appeal on that station, at least among the younger set was called *Spinner's Sanctum* and the disc jockey was Jay Allen Brimmer. It aired in the evenings and was a call-in show, where you could actually hear yourself on the radio as you requested a certain tune for your favorite gal or guy. A song that particularly appealed to us Greenlee children was called "Slap 'Er down Again, Paw."

Daddy, who was quite particular with the family name, and did not want it bandied about in connection with these sorts of songs, got quite upset when he would hear that that song had been requested by one of the Greenlee children in Eustis. In deference to his feelings, we stopped using our names, but we didn't stop requesting the silly song!

WLBE later moved from Eustis to its longstanding home on Silver Lake near Leesburg. After the departure of **WLBE**, another station made Eustis its home. **WLCO** came along in about 1950 I reckon, and was located in Eustis Heights near Livingston's Packing House.

I recall that **WLCO** had a promotion in which they would announce that a call would be made to one of the Golden Triangle towns. And if the one answering that call would say ***"WLCO, 1240 on the dial"*** a cash prize would be awarded! Well, folks, I was listening one day and hoping that someday the call would come to our house on Barnes Avenue! And behold! The announcer said that he was calling a number in Eustis. You could hear him dialing it! And... our phone rang! Could it be?

I answered the phone as instructed, and sure enough, I was the winner of $15.00! It might as well have been $500.00 to me! That may have been the only money I have ever won!

72

A Family of Storm-Chasers

We Greenlees loved stormy weather! I'm not sure how that ever came to be, but hurricane season was one of excitement for us! And even now, the days that invigorate me more than any others are overcast, rainy and windy! Lightning and thunder are my friends, too.

Sometime in the mid-1940s, shortly after we had moved to Barnes Avenue from Belmont Heights, the radio began to warn us that we were in the path of a hurricane that was coming directly up the center of the state! Friends, ole Jamie here (along with John, Miriam, Mama and Daddy) could hardly contain himself! Our "hatches were all battened down" and we eagerly awaited the storm!

Bad news soon came to us, however. That storm decided to veer toward the east coast when just below Orlando, and it began to head for Indian River City! We were only going to get a little breeze from it! Well, folks, it didn't take long for our family to pile into that old Model A Ford and head for Orlando! When we arrived there it was quite stormy, but we turned off Orange Blossom Trail onto Highway 50 that would take us toward Indian River City.

The weather got dramatically worse as we drove east. The rain was coming down hard and the wind was rocking that old car, but we carried on. Finally we reached a spot where the heavy rain was causing water to come over the road to a depth that it was beginning to choke the engine down. Daddy saw the importance at that time of us being able to return home safely. So reluctantly the Greenlees turned around and headed back to Eustis.

We have had several hurricanes come through where we now live in central North Carolina, and I must admit to some excitement as they come through. I reckon that little boy in me will be around as long as I am!

73

Score: Tuppy – 1, Mr. Coral Snake - 0

Cats played a big role in our young lives. Can't remember a time when we did not have at least one, and often more than one. Daddy was a cat-lover from his childhood. Mama, however, only tolerated having them around I reckon to keep peace in the family. Actually, after we children were all gone, she did have a favorite little kitty. But my vignette here concerns a highly unusual event that might well border on being a miracle in the life of our cat named Tuppy.

As you probably know, an occasional Coral snake is seen in Central Florida. It was about 1949 when Tuppy brought one of those varmints home! We children were horrified to see that multi-colored snake hanging out both sides of Tuppy's mouth, and very much alive! As the Greenlee family attempted to make the cat and the snake part company, the worst possible outcome happened!

Tuppy turned his attention to us instead of Mr. Coral Snake, and the snake bit him on his neck! Well, he let go of the snake at this point, and tore out running to the back yard and got up under the back porch. We made short work of the snake, and ran to see what we could do for our doomed cat! Now, our daddy was a cat-lover first class, and it broke his heart to see Tuppy lying under there with labored breathing. But being a realist and knowing that the venom from a Coral snake is among the deadliest of them all, he decided to go on to work, saying that when he came home for lunch he would bury Tuppy.

Lunchtime came and so did Daddy. And he found that Tuppy was still breathing but not much else. So he elected to euthanize the cat. He bought some chloroform, soaked a rag in it, and put the cat and the rag under a cardboard box. The fumes given off by that substance are deadly and would mercifully end the ebbing life of our pet.

After a more than sufficient time under the box, Daddy removed it to find Tuppy standing up! He was glassy-eyed and barely breathing as he fell over on his side. Next thing to dead, he was. So Daddy said that when he got home from work in the evening he would bury Tuppy. And folks, what happened after this made the newspapers!

When Daddy got home, Tuppy was out front to meet him as usual! Coral snake venom and chloroform could not kill that cat! Could it be that the chloroform fumes served as an antitoxin for the venom? Don't know, but I remember that we had our pet Tuppy for a number of years after that close call.

There were side-effects however. They included Tuppy being deaf and having no sense of smell or taste. But his miraculous survival made both the Eustis Lake Region News and the Orlando Sentinel.

74

My Encounter with Baseball Great Ted Williams

I know I have mentioned that I was born a Boston Red Sox fan. Don't know why, you know, way down there in Eustis and all. That's a long way from Boston. But my dream of actually seeing the Red Sox play a game had a chance of coming true once a year during Spring Training.

The Washington Senators trained in Orlando. And once during that Spring-training season Boston would come to town for a game. Daddy, knowing my love for the Sox, took John and me to the game once. Folks, heaven could not possibly hold any more delights than what I experienced at that game! I saw my heroes: Ted Williams, Dom DiMaggio, Al Zarilla, Johnny Pesky, Bobby Doerr, Walt Dropo, Birdie Tebbitts and Vern Stephens and an array of great pitchers like Mel Parnell, Mickey McDermott and Ellis Kinder. (Just having fun naming some of those I remember!).

But the event that I will remember all of my days is what took place between one of the innings. Boston had taken the field but the inning had not started. Now, I had a Brownie Hawkeye camera and that helped birth a great idea. Why not jump out of those stands and just run down the left field line to where Ted Williams stood? I could snap him up close and get back before the game commenced again.

Folks, that's what I did. On impulse I bailed out and my little short legs were working hard to get me out to where Ted was. Seemed like a mile, but when I got there I yelled, "Hey Ted!" I reckon he had already seen me coming anyhow. But he turned to face me, posing while the Hawkeye snapped a picture! I was interacting with The Splendid Splinter, the greatest hitter in major league baseball, Ted Williams!

It was a small thing for Ted to do, but his generosity absolutely made me the happiest kid in Eustis for some time! I treasured that picture until after I had joined the Air Force. Sadly, sometime in those early Air Force years, the picture was inadvertently thrown away.

When game day rolled around the next year, the folks thought it might be better for me to get permission from the principal of Eustis High School to be absent from school that afternoon. Bad mistake! Mr. Godbold told me absolutely not! Uncharacteristically for this seventh grader, I roared back at him "AND WHY NOT?" Did that come out of my mouth? He was not amused by my smart retort and I came within an inch of receiving the business end of his paddle!

So no ball game but also no sore rear end from Mr. Godbold's paddle. Ya know, in some ways maybe I broke even!

75

My Brother, My Role Model

When the new First Baptist Church building at the corner of Prescott and Orange was still under construction, conditions were such within the congregation at that time that a fairly large segment began to hold services in it. I recall the rows of folding chairs sitting on unfinished floors. A piano had been brought in and it sat to the left of the front; it seems like there was a small unfinished room that contained it, and it could be seen between the studs.

And sometimes something special took place when it came time for music. The pianist, Frances Polk, would be accompanied by my brother John playing the violin! I can't remember just what prompted John to take up the violin. But I think maybe he was impressed by a Christian violinist named Carlos Pergalis (also known as Franz Gruber, I believe). Anyhow, John became quite a violinist for a mid-teen and frequently played it in church services. I was proud of that.

I suppose that it is normal for younger siblings to look up to their elder ones. John is 20 months older than me, and was a grade ahead in school. We are close enough in age that we participated in many things together. And I have realized through the years, I reckon it has been a growing realization, that I actually saw in John a lot of what and who I wanted to be. He was gifted in the musical field, playing not only the violin, but the bass clarinet and the sousaphone (tuba). When the time came in my later high school years that I needed some extra credits, I joined the EHS band and of course I wanted to play the tuba.

John was an excellent softball player in those days, too. Folks, that brother of mine could hit! It is quite possible that I acquired my great love for softball from him. I think I was more excited than him when he broke Babe Ruth's home run record, hitting 61 home runs (ball had to fly over Barnes Avenue and the power wires in left field on our ball field beside the house, to be a homer…quite a poke!). My love for softball has followed me through the years. (At 70 years old I still know where my fielder's glove is, and will toss the ball anytime!)

In our growing up years I often wished that I had John's temperament. He never seemed to let many things worry him. On the other hand, I was a basket full of nervous stomachs! And he seemed to always know what he wanted to do and be. I watched with much pride as he went off with a band scholarship to Florida State University, where he completed his degree early and entered a business that he is still pursuing today.

Our paths have gone in different directions, and the miles separate us now. But we do our best to have a reunion once a year, usually near Christmas, meeting in the town of our births, Bartow, Florida, for a few hours. Just a word of appreciation for my brother and the lessons he taught me.

76

"Rat Day" Fears

I'm sure that Eustis High School does not observe "Rat Day" anymore! But in the early 1950s it was a time-honored tradition. Rat Day? It was a school-sanctioned day set aside to allow the seniors to demean and degrade the freshmen, all in the name of fun! Usually a senior would choose a freshman, and would require him or her to do stuff like carry the senior's books to each class. I reckon it was a rite of passage into high school for the freshmen. And as long as it didn't get out of hand, the freshmen suffered through it knowing that their turn would come when they were seniors.

Well, as long as that was all there was to it, okay. But in some cases it got a little too confrontational. And that is exactly what this little freshman guy was afraid of. There was a senior fella that enjoyed picking on me. Nothing too bad, but I was afraid of him. And he kept warning me that I was "gunna be toast" on Rat Day!

The night before Rat Day I did not sleep. In fact I threw up. And I cried while admitting to Mama that I was afraid to go to school because of what I feared the day would bring. She asked if I wanted to stay home; after all, I had been sick in the night. But I knew that I had to face up to what the rest of the freshmen were having to face.

So off to EHS I went. And this Rat Day was not as bad as I had conjured it up to be. The guy had me do some things like push a pencil with my nose all the way down the aisle in the auditorium. And after making some fun of me and a few of his derisive and embarrassing remarks coming at me, the day turned into a routine one.

I had the feeling that most of the freshmen actually liked the antics and eagerly looked forward to the day that the shoe would be on the other foot. But I never enjoyed that kind of interplay. And when I was a senior the freshman I chose was a lucky one! I hope he remembered that when he became a senior!

77

The Wrong Girl

Here is a bad Post Office arcade experience for me…and for some poor, unsuspecting lady who was minding her own business! As you probably know by now, my dad's shoe repair shop was in the arcade of the Eustis Post Office when it was located at the intersection of Eustis Street and Orange Avenue in 1949. And though it was taboo, some of us boys rode our bicycles around in that place from time to time! The Postmaster did not like it but I still did a bit of it.

Germane to this story is the fact that friend and classmate, Linda, and I used to punch each other on the arm, actually pretty hard! I'm not sure what that might represent to a psychologist, but he would probably be right. Anyhow, on with the episode.

As I came wheeling into the Post Office who should I spy at the window talking to a postal clerk, but Linda! Aha! She did not see me and here was a chance to lay a good one on her arm as I rode by her! I picked up speed on my Firestone bike and passing just behind her, I landed a fist solidly on her upper arm just below her shoulder! You could hear the "smack" all over the lobby! Boy, did I score one there!

My punch, however, was followed by a loud groan from a voice unfamiliar to me! When I finally got stopped and looked back, a strange woman was glaring at me and holding on to her shoulder! It was not my friend Linda! The gent behind the counter was saying, "Did he hit you with that bicycle?" She moaned, "No…With his fist!"

Man, I was one scared little dude! I had no idea how to proceed from that point, but instinct told me I needed to go apologize to her. White as a sheet, I am sure, I pushed my bike back to where she stood and stammered out how sorry I was and that the punch had been intended for a friend of mine that she resembled from the back! I don't remember her response but I guarantee that it was not a pleasantry. I then high-tailed it out of that arcade and headed for Barnes Avenue.

I reckon Daddy did not get yelled at by the Postmaster, because I never heard any more about the incident. Today I am sure I would be hauled into juvenile court and my family sued over this event. Glad I grew up in the 50s.

Any morals in this episode? A couple. Kids, don't ride your bikes inside of Public Buildings. And if you are gunna punch some girl you like, make sure it's her before you swing that fist! (I learned somewhat later that there were much better ways to show affection!)

78

Falling for the Girls

In the late 1940s we still cooked on a kerosene stove. It seemed to me to work just fine, but from time to time it needed a refill. I had been asked to take the 1-gallon kerosene can and go to Hunsucker's Gas Station to purchase some. H. S. Hunsucker's station was 5 blocks down Grove Street from our house on Barnes Avenue.

So I mounted my trusty (except for the brakes) Firestone bike, headed down the clay road that Barnes Avenue was in those days, and turned onto Grove Street. Now folks, I have alluded to the fact that I was a shy boy in those days, especially when the opposite sex was involved. But shyness does not mean a lack of interest in girls. I could appreciate a girl with looks even if from a distance.

Well, as I turned on to Grove, I noticed three quite comely lasses who were a couple of years ahead of me in school, on bicycles coming on Grove just behind me. Cute? I reckon so! And one more look would not hurt a thing! So with empty kerosene can clanging against my front fender as it dangled from my handlebars, I casually looked back over my shoulder. Man, what a smooth move. And yep, cute all right.

Okay, now let me set the stage for this strange event in my young life. Coming in my direction was an automobile about a block away, near Atwater Avenue. I tell you this because the very next thing I remember after taking that look back at the girls was getting up off the road! Right! The girls were standing around me and the car was backing up to see if I was hurt!

I do not remember one thing about falling from the bike or hitting the road! But it must have been a doozie of a wreck to get the attention of the motorist too! I reckon I was unconscious for a few moments, and did have some scrapes from meeting Mr. Grove Street. The kerosene can had a pretty good dent in it, too. I was shaken up badly but otherwise in pretty good shape. And while I appreciated the attention I was receiving from these young ladies, there was someone else I needed to see at that time.

I returned to home and my mama to get a little sympathy from her. After some TLC and the cleaning of my contusions, I was off again to Hunsucker's with no looking back at girls! But to this day I do not know what happened there. I feel sure the car did not hit me. But either that kerosene can got tangled up in my steering, causing an immediate crash or else I simply passed out!

Passing out because of a second look at some girls? Nah! Girls might have caused me to do some things but passing out was not one of them! It had to be the kerosene can.

Moral: Don't let your "can" get too near the operating parts of your bicycle, especially when your gaze is anywhere but on the road ahead.

79

The Death of Spotty

Every kid needs to have a pet they can feel like is his or her very own. In my case it was Spotty, a pup from some source that I cannot remember. He came to our household and into my life in 1944. He was a Heinz dog, white with a couple of large brown spots, a mixture of 57 varieties no doubt. And we were fast friends from the beginning.

In those days most non-pedigree dogs had the freedom to roam the neighborhoods, poop wherever they wanted to and play with or sometimes fight other dogs of those families living around you. (The only time we ever shut our female dog up was when she was in heat.) There were no fence laws and few chains. But the dogs knew where they lived and would be home at mealtimes and to sleep in the yard somewhere. And we got along fine in the neighborhood.

But not having Spotty confined at least to our yard by some restraint became his downfall and early demise. And I had the traumatic experience to be on hand when it happened. Spotty was a car-chaser. On that fateful day, the car of a neighbor living several blocks away came noisily down Barnes Avenue, a cloud of dust from the clay road rolling out from behind it. Ahh, Spotty! It was just asking to be chased, wasn't it?

The car was not traveling at such speed that Spotty could not catch up to it. In fact he passed the car and ended up in front of it. I don't think the neighbor ever knew that the dog was there and he did not slow down. Spotty was not nimble enough to elude the front tire and under it he went with a terrifying yelllllllp! The car continued down the road and turned onto Grove Street. Spotty's life was ending in front of my horrified eyes! A few labored breaths and whimpers and he was gone.

In those days our vacant lot had an old oak tree standing in the far corner near the road. Daddy buried Spotty near that tree. Each one of us has a way of expressing grief and they are not all the same. I think that I was the only one of the family members that did not shed a tear. I wanted to, but they would not come. This little boy dealt with his grief differently. Daddy had fixed us a rope swing in that oak tree, and I would sit in that swing for lengthy periods of time making up sad songs to sing about Spotty.

My way at that particular time must have been right for me. For in just a little while summer night campouts and softball games were again taking place right over the erstwhile hallowed spot where my pet lay.

80

Light in the Darkness

Must have been in the late 1940s. Being at home alone after dark was not my favorite thing to do as a young lad of 11 or so. And I almost never was for any lengthy time, as brother John and sister Miriam were usually there. But not this time. It was the season of the year when darkness comes early and Daddy and Mama would not be home from work before the oncoming night. This would make me a bit uncomfortable. Not unbearably so, save for this exception: not only was it late enough for darkness but there was also a violent lightning storm in progress!

As I sat rather nervously on the sofa trying to keep my mind on things more pleasant, suddenly a fierce bolt of lightning flashed accompanied by an instantaneous clap of deafening thunder! And folks, I found myself in total darkness! A fuse had blown!

After the initial shock and accompanying terror had abated somewhat, I began to decide the best course of action to take. I knew of no flashlight that we might have in the house. But there was a kerosene lamp out on the back porch. I could light that lamp if only I could find the matches in what was basically total darkness. And then I remembered that matches were kept in the bathroom medicine cabinet. They may have been put there to hide them from us kids, but I knew where they were.

So I groped my way into the bathroom and turned on the light. I found the matches and went to the back porch and turned on the light. I retrieved the lamp and lit it. You might have noticed several things by this time. It did not occur to this bright boy that I had turned lights on in the house to help me find the matches and the lamp! Only after the lamp was burning, did I realize that not all of the electricity was off in the house! I had been using it! Duhhhhhh…

The house on Barnes Avenue was actually an early duplex, and it was equipped with two electrical systems. Only one screw-in fuse had blown; the other was functioning just fine! Shoot, with the light on I could and did replace the bad fuse, and light blessed the entire house again!

I marveled at my lack of perception, or at least my being so slow on the uptake in this case. It took awhile for me to tell the folks about this incident. Heck, I didn't want to further shake their confidence in my good sense! And now I've told you, too, but about 60 years separates me from that incident. (Don't let it get around, but sometimes this end of my life looks a lot like that other end!)

Don't go lookin' for screw-in fuses, kids. You won't find 'em!

81

Ted, the Family Friend

During my growing up years, I do not remember my parents ever having friends to our house on any regular basis, either at Belmont Heights or in Eustis. They were on friendly terms with all of our neighbors but visits back and forth were rare if at all. Outside of the two church families we were connected with, the socializing was pretty much left to us children. I think it may have been that way in most of our friend's homes, too.

An exception to the above was Ted Parker. From my earliest memories Ted was a frequent visitor in our home. He was unmarried in the early days, and Daddy would go and pick him up from his home on Grove Street and bring him out to Belmont Heights and later to our home on Barnes Avenue. Ted and the folks spent untold hours visiting and playing dominoes.

Ted was the Christmas Card man in Eustis. Each year he would take orders from the Eustis folks and supply them with quality greeting cards. I remember Daddy telling of Ted's complaining about the cost of the cards. He once told daddy that his profit margin was getting smaller each year, and he needed a way to drum up more customers.

Daddy, with a straight face, said "Ted, I have an idea. Sell 'em for a dollar a box!" Ted, always ready to fall for one of Dad's jokes, said, "Herb! I'd lose my shirt! I'd lose money on each box!" Daddy came back with, "But Ted, you would offset that loss with the volume of business you would get!" After a moment's contemplation of Dad's statement, Ted said, "HERB!!" Not sure if he thought Daddy was serious at first. Heck, he just might have figured Daddy was a little light in his business sense department.

Ted and Dad remained fast friends until Ted's death some years later. Back to the socializing department for a moment. We Greenlee children certainly did have many friends to the house numerous times! The house on Barnes Avenue was often filled with schoolmates and neighborhood kids of all ages. We fielded softball teams in the lot beside the house for after-school games, with enough players on each side to make a game of it. There were sleep-overs both in the house and camping in tents in the lot or in our log cabin playhouse. We were blessed with times of great entertainment furnished mostly by Daddy that included hamburger fry's for all the kids around in the long summer evenings and at Halloween!

And though Mama was often in the background of the goings-on, without her help many of the aforementioned things would not have taken place. We were blessed children.

Remember the good things of your childhood, folks, and do likewise for your offspring!

82

The Death of Gonga

If one would catch a more accurate glimpse into my growing up process, it would have to include occasions of sadness. I relate a "biggie" for me and my family in this episode.

It was on a warm July night in 1948 when the Greenlee tribe had just returned from a town-team softball game at Eustis High School. As we were entering the house the phone rang. And our evening of lighthearted family fun suddenly turned into stunned disbelief that usually precedes the coming to terms with terrible news.

A telephone operator calling from the exchange in Orlando told Daddy, "I have a telegram from Mary: 'Mama died today. Come quickly.'" I think she repeated it twice at Daddy's request. I recall vividly the shock of the moment. Mama throwing herself across her bed and sobbing. Daddy consoling Mama while considering what he had to do to get the old Ford ready for a 90-mile trip through the night to Bartow.

John, Miriam and I were certainly grieving at the loss of "Gonga." Gonga was our beloved grandmother who would be there forever for us. That death would take that dear person was unthinkable, and I know I never considered it. But as for me, my greatest concern was about how this was affecting my mother. Mama had never really cut her apron strings from her mother in Bartow.

Often we spent time in Bartow. For some years, except in school terms, we would spend one week out of each month there, so I was told. I know it must be true because we children considered Gonga's house our second home.

After hastily packing some clothes, we set out for whatever would await us in three hours. I did my best to console my mother on that seemingly endless trip. It was a relief to arrive and have Grandpa, Uncle Buddy, Aunt Rachel and Aunt Mary and our cousins to share in grief and consolation with Mama and us.

This was the first death of a family member that I really felt a "heart string" connection to. Daddy's grandfather had died in our home that same year, and though I loved him, the bond that I, along with John and Miriam, had with Gonga was without compare.

The funeral came and went, and we, especially Mama, began to adjust to life without precious Gonga. It was a slow process for her. It seems that our trips to Bartow became less frequent. And some weeks passed before Daddy gave Mama a letter that had come from Gonga on the day she had died. She had told Mama in it that she had been having some chest pains for awhile, "like a hot needle that starts near the front of my chest and stabs all the way to my back."

I know that everyone undergoes profound moments of grief, some lasting longer than others. I have suffered through many now at my age, but the first one came when I was eleven. Gonga was special.

83

School Report I Didn't Give

I was in the third grade, Nell Fite's class. So that would make it late 1945 or early 1946. All of us in the class were expected to read a report to the class that we had written on various subjects. Mine was to be about American Indians. Somehow though, my report was not coming together! My stress level was becoming obvious to my father.

I remember that we were in his shoe repair shop in the post office arcade, when he offered to help me with the report. So with pencil and paper in hand, I began to take down what Daddy was dictating to me. And so help me, he was giving me information on a first grade level! Even though I was only a couple of years past that grade level, I found his information far beneath the learning norm for third-graders! Now, my daddy was a very intelligent man, but he was totally misreading my learning level.

Not wanting to hurt his feelings, I dutifully wrote down what he offered. When finished, I thanked him for his help and folded the paper. Tomorrow was the day! How could I possibly read that report to the class? I would be the laughing stock for sure! And I certainly had nothing else to offer.

I sure hated to go to school that day (more than usual!). I sat squirming as report after report was being read. My turn was coming! And it was here! "James, stand up and read your report to the class." Folks, that report was folded and crumpled in my pocket. And I became a liar right there. I told Miss Fite that I did not have a report! She scolded me for not having my assignment and told me my grade would suffer because of it.

But my bad day was not over! Each day I would go from the Eustis Elementary School to Daddy's shoe shop after school! "He's gunna ask me how the report went!" What would I tell him? The report was still crumpled in my pocket!

I had to get rid of that report. Daddy must never see it again! As I reached the Post Office arcade entrance on Orange Avenue I noticed a very small gap where the concrete sidewalk met the building. The folded report slipped very nicely into that little crevice and went out of sight! Okay, that is done. Now comes the hard part: Seeing Daddy!

Sure enough, his first question concerned the report. Again I lied. "It went good, Daddy! Thanks!" I felt guilty for my untruthful answers, for I was brought up to know what sin is! I reckon I was employing "situation ethics" before I even had a name for it (ha). And I cannot tell you how many times afterward that I stopped and looked carefully to make sure that report was remaining hidden in the crevice! (Wonder if that report is still under that concrete where the entrance used to be...)

84

Miriam's Daring Venture

And then there was a night in the very early 1950s when my sister Miriam and several other slumber party participants decided it would be fun to walk to downtown in their night clothes. Yes. At the midnight hour when most were sleeping, these young teen girls slipped out from one of their houses, and headed up Grove Street. Traffic was sparse and they were able to scramble into front yards and get behind trees and hedges when cars did come by.

Well, folks, these girls (I think there were three) did make it to the streets of our Eustis business district, about a mile away. And there they met with a not-so-friendly police officer who took them into custody. I can't remember if he loaded them into his squad car and escorted them home, or if he called parents to come pick them up. And I'm not privy to what happened to the other girls, but Miriam's parents were not amused by this terribly dangerous venture! As far as I know, this never happened again. Or at least, they didn't get caught if it did!

Sleepovers at the Greenlee household for Miriam and her friends took place on the screened front porch. It was a rather secluded spot behind two large bushes and with wood sides waist high. It was safe enough, especially with my parent's bedroom just inside the door. But their cutting up and giggling for half the night did not make sleep time in our little house a pleasant time, at least for me.

John and I had our friends overnight in tents in the lot next door. Though I did a fair amount of this "camping out", I can't say that it ranked among my favorite things to do. But we did have times of fun, and we didn't disturb any sleepers in the Greenlee household.

85

The Purloined Cigarettes

In the late 1940s, my uncle Buddy drove a LaSalle, I believe it to be a 1939 model. (The LaSalle was made by General Motors and was a relative of the Cadillac.) Uncle Buddy had made the trip from Bartow to visit us. So there was this good-lookin' car pulled into our front yard just waiting to be explored by a couple of young teen boys.

Sitting in the vehicle, my friend and I were looking at the various buttons and things, when we decided to look in the glove compartment. Uncle Buddy was a smoker, and there before our eyes was an unopened pack of cigarettes! To this day I do not know what possessed us, but we took that pack from the car. Shoot, neither one of us had any experience with cigarettes at that time! (I must take blame for the theft…I no doubt instigated it. Reckon I thought he would never miss 'em!)

What to do now with our purloined "treasure"? Well, out in the vacant lot next to the house, we boys had dug a very large hole, big enough for us to get into. It was partially covered with boards, and made a nice albeit snug little clubhouse. So we got in the hole and dug out a little tunnel-like hole in the side of it. There we placed the cigarettes, and we covered the hole over so that just my buddy and I would know where they were.

So far so good! I did not know what we would do with the smokes and I guess we might have even returned them to the glove compartment after awhile, as our consciences would let us know we had done wrong. But when we went back in just a little while to retrieve them, the dampness in the soil had caused the pack to burst open! Too late! So my friend took the evidence with him as he left for home, and I went into the house, hoping against hope that Uncle Buddy would not need those cigarettes!

Wrong! I watched with dismay as he left the family group on the front porch to retrieve his cigarettes from the car. I saw him rummaging around in the glove compartment. And then he came back in, in amazement! "I know I put a new pack of cigarettes in that glove box," he said. Some discussion began to take place about this. I was not part of that discussion, I assure you!

Then I was brought into it. Hadn't my friend and I been in the car earlier? I answered yes. Did you see the cigarettes? I answered ashamedly, "yes." Had I taken the cigarettes? I owned up to that fact, too. Where were they now? I explained what had happened, implicating only myself. Uncle Buddy wanted to just forget it. But Mom and Dad were not so quick to do so. Daddy gave me 30 cents to give to Uncle Buddy and I asked his forgiveness for what I had done.

It's the little incidents along the way in our childhoods that help to mold our character. This, among others, remains a part of my memory.

86

Panic in the Operating Room

My grandson had his tonsils taken out several days ago. He is recovering nicely and rapidly. His surgery brought to mind my own, when I was 4 years old. That would make it late 1941 or early 1942 while we lived in Belmont Heights. In my case, Mama and Daddy worried about me because I didn't seem to have the energy that a kid my age should have. I have been told that I could play for only a few minutes before coming inside and lying down for awhile.

Doctor Louis Bowen's diagnosis called for an immediate tonsillectomy. He feared for my life if those infected glands didn't come out. So, it was off to Bartow where Mama always returned when things of importance took place. I reckon it was old Doctor Murphy that performed the surgery, the same one that had delivered me four years earlier.

I do remember the absolute terror of that day as we arrived at Bartow General Hospital. I refused to get out of the car, and when Mama finally got her arms around me to forcibly remove me, I pinched her under the chin so hard that she carried a bruise for months.

The horror continued when in the operating room, Mama had to leave me. While I screamed for her, I recall the mask being slipped over my entire face. It was padded around the edge and there was wire mesh almost like screen wire that formed the mask. I can to this day remember the smell of the ether that they used in those days, as it was dripped onto the mask. And then…I was waking up!

The recovery period in those days was a few days longer than now. But recover I did, and all the ice cream and attention received during that time made the horror of the event itself abate somewhat. I guess that that was the first time though, that I ever recall experiencing absolute panic! There would be more to come in the years ahead, and I reckon it helped me to realize that life goes on after the trauma is over!

87

My Possum Confrontation

A neighbor of ours on Barnes Avenue during our earlier years there (probably 1943-1947), had a tree cleaning service. Mr. Hammond would clean the Spanish moss from the trees of Eustis, and would then "process" it for sale.

Mr. Hammond would harvest the moss for a price, of course, and then would hang it out on long wires connected to posts in the field beside his house and across from our house. Something I learned as a child was that the moss, a parasite, will die unless connected to a source of nourishment, usually the many oaks in our yards of Eustis. So after quite some time of "drying out", the outer coating of the moss would sluff off, leaving a tough slim fiber. This fiber Mr. Hammond sold to furniture manufacturers for stuffing in pillows and sofas.

It was common for us to hear and then see Mr. Hammond coming in his ancient little truck, loaded to overflowing with moss. I reckon that there were other folks doing this same thing, but Mr. Hammond is the only one I ever knew that did.

The Hammonds also had chickens and ducks. One day Mrs. Hammond came to our house and asked me to come over and get a possum out of one of her hen's nests. Shoot, I didn't know anything about dealing with a possum! And I was not anxious to get face to face with one!

So I waddled in a squat position into the rather close environment of her chicken coop to where the nest was located. And sure enough, the offending opossum was ensconced on it. So here I was, all hunched down and in a "stand-off" with the varmint. Folks, the possum was grinning at me, but I knew he did not plan to exchange pleasantries. What the heck was I doing in there?

I had brought a good size stick in with me to prod him with, hoping he would decide to leave on his own. But a few timid prods only brought a bigger grin, if you know what I mean! He was not leaving! In fact it looked like he wanted to take me on! I was afraid that if I should turn around and try to leave the coop, he would attack me from behind. So this scared little boy turned that stick around so the little end was in my hand. Then with all my might I whacked that possum on the head! Thank the Lord that was all it took! It could have enraged him and I would have been victim of a possum attack! But it killed him!

I felt kinda sorry but it turned into either him or me…and I had made sure it was him! So I dragged him out of the chicken coop by his tail and buried him in Mrs. Hammond's front yard. She was grateful to me and gave me a couple of duck eggs, but it took me awhile to get over it. It's good to see that most possums confine their wanderings to the roads of our nation now.

88

Early Sneakin' and Smokin'

Baseball was my love as you have found out in my writings. And my buddies and I loved to attend the town team games at the Eustis Baseball Park near the Eustis Airport. In fact, several of us developed a real affinity for the old ball park! And it was not just because of the game itself!

When the field was not in use, the gates were locked. But we found that to be no deterrent as we would enter the facilities on the day after a game. What did we find intriguing in that place? Cigarette butts! Right!

We would scrounge up all the butts that still had some good smokin' size about them. And if they had one, we would tear off the filter (filters were just coming into being) and the burnt end. We would put that end in our mouths and light up!

Of course I would come home after these sessions smelling like a pool hall on Saturday night! I knew Mama would catch me. I could see her sniff the air as I came by her. Then she would say, "Jamie, let me smell your breath!" Now folks, I learned a little trick when it comes to "breath smellin'". If you open your mouth and inhale through it, it makes the same sound as if you are exhaling. Try it and see!

So I passed my breath test. But alas, the smell was usually so strong on my clothes that she would ask me point blank if I had been smoking. I could not lie to Mama. I don't know how many times we went through this little scenario, with each time her telling me if she caught me again she would have to tell Daddy. She never did.

Don't know how I escaped the clutches of a cigarette habit, but though I dabbled throughout my early life with them I never developed a habit and haven't smoked at all for 22 years as I write in the year 2009.

89

The Bugs of Barnes Avenue

Let's call this one "The Bugs of Barnes Avenue." Our aging wooden house on Barnes Avenue was a safe haven for roaches of all kinds! They lived and bred inside of the walls! Especially the walls on the back porch where my "bedroom area" was. No matter the bug spray used, they were pretty much a part of our lives. Particularly offensive were the shiny, black ones that would give off a sweetish odor when disturbed. We called 'em cockroaches but I have heard them called wood roaches, too.

Once my sister Miriam had gone in to the bathroom and smelled one of those cockroaches. She came storming out of there and in to the kitchen where Mama was. "Mama, I am not going back in that bathroom until somebody goes in there and finds that roach and kills it!" Mama looked up from what she was doing, and saw on the very top of the head of her precious but upset daughter, the offending cockroach!

Moving calmly so as to not startle either Miriam or the roach, Mama suddenly slapped a dish towel across her head that instantly ended the life of the roach and sent Miriam into a hissy fit! It took awhile for her to get over the fact that she had actually transported that vile bug on her person! We all laughed about it later – much later for Miriam.

Also we had a continuing supply of those "flying roaches!" I don't know how I ever slept with those airborne terror-bugs fluttering across the porch and hitting the walls so hard you could hear them smack it! Well, they were particularly active one night, and as usual I had my sheet pulled up over my head with just my nose protruding! Never can be too safe in the roach arena! And folks, one of those varmints landed right on my nose! I had no idea that I could actually rise up from the bed and land with my feet on the floor in one simple move and moment!

Another curious bug we had, and one that I have not seen anywhere before or since, was the grampus! We had a few of these fierce-looking ugly black varmints in our basement and under the house from time to time. A grampus is a segmented bug like an ant, but is 3-4 inches long! It has pinchers on the front like a scorpion and a long needle sticking up from it's rear end. Didn't know what a grampus would do to me if it ever caught me, but I never gave one the chance!

90

Mama, a Great Christian Example

The occasion was the 125th birthday of my hometown, Eustis, Florida. Wife Sylvia and I had come from North Carolina to be there for the events of February 22 and 23, 2008. A reception was given at the school for all of the Eustis High School graduates, and we attended hoping to see many of my old classmates. Although some were there, most were not, which was a disappointment for me. But I did see my high school baseball coach!

Bill Kelsey remembered me (so he said) and we had a nice chat. And there were a scattering of others that I had seen more recently than 1955. But one lady, upon finding out who I was, began to tell me about the influence that my mother, Kathleen, had had on her life.

She said that Mama had been her Sunday School teacher at the First Baptist Church for several years when she was in junior high school. She related that Mama had worn the same green print dress every Sunday during those years. She had watched as the dress became frayed and had seen where Mama had patched and sewn it up. It was obvious that it was the only Sunday dress Mama had. Though it was never talked about, Mama's emphasis on what

was really important as shown by her great Bible teaching gave this young lady a lesson about life.

For she said that she too had only one dress to wear a lot of the time as a child, having to accept hand-me-downs when they were available. But she was able to hold her head high, remembering that her Sunday School teacher had demonstrated that beauty was not in what clothed the body. She wanted me to know that Mama had made a difference in her life.

John, Miriam and I had a very special mother.

91

Sleepover Skullduggery

Just after my brother John had headed out to Florida State University in the fall of 1954, his bedroom became mine. I gladly moved into his room – the converted kitchen of the duplex unit on the left side of the house. (Our house on Barnes Avenue had been a duplex prior to our moving to it.) For several years my bedroom had been a curtained-off area of the back porch, and though it did me okay, I was grateful for a "real" room!

My sister Miriam had occasional sleep overs with her friends, and due to the smallness of our house, the only place suitable for them to sleep was on the front porch. It was safe enough with the latched screen door and secluded enough behind two large arborvitae bushes, and close to my parents' bedroom should trouble arise.

Teenage boys often wonder what teenage girls talk about when they have things like sleep overs. Well, curiosity would sometimes overcome me in those late hours. I could hear muffled talking and giggling clear back to my room. So, I would carefully open the back door and creep along the outside of the house until I was right beside the porch. And I listened. They would have killed me if they had known about my spying missions and my whereabouts just feet from them.

Some things I learned on those missions would best not be repeated to any reader, and I found that the subject matter was a lot like that of teenage boys at their sleep overs! And you know, although they did not know of my escapades, they inadvertently got even with me one night. It must have been 3 o'clock in the morning when I woke from a sound sleep with something all over me and my bed!

Miriam and her friends had snuck through the house, got a box of salt from the kitchen, and had come in to my room with it. They poured most of the contents of that box all over me! I was a sticky salty mess! And I might add, highly enraged that my privacy had been violated! But after a bath and a change of sheets, I began to cool down a little, realizing that my "sin" and now their "sin" had pretty well canceled each other out!

Ahh, but they never knew of my "sin" until perhaps now should one of them read this! If so, Sorrreeee!

92

My Checkered BB Gun History

BB Guns! Which boy did not have one? If you were strong enough to cock one of those Red Ryder's, you were old enough to have one. Gun safety, at least for the BB gun crowd, was not high on the list of things important for kids to know. At least that's the way it seemed to this kid!

There were a couple of brothers that lived on Atwater Avenue, who were older than me. The older one had gotten a new BB gun. Now when one wants to test his skills with a gun, what is better than a moving target? Right. Nothing. This was in the early days before the house next to ours on Barnes Avenue had been built, say 1945. That vacant lot held intrigue for me in that there were several gopher holes amongst the weeds. I had set my gopher traps earlier and had gone to check for a trapped gopher (that never was there).

Suddenly I felt a sharp stinging pain on my calf! Before I could react to that pain another just like it hit the other leg! I looked and there was that new gun owner shooting BBs at me as fast as he could re-cock it. Actually he must have been a pretty good shot, as he was maybe 100 feet from me. I remember him laughing as I whooped it up and headed for our house and my mama! He got his "come-uppence" after my mama visited his mama, and I soon felt secure in checking my gopher traps again.

But it's a wonder that more eyes were not put out and other injuries caused by accidental BB gun firings. I shot one of my best friends in the neck one time by accident, and though it did not break the skin, he took great umbrage at the incident. I would mention his name now, but I don't want to get that started all over again!

One thing we boys liked to do was try to shoot birds sitting on the power lines on Barnes Avenue. Heck, the safest place one of those birds could possibly be when I was shooting was on the wire that I was aiming at.

But the last time I ever used my BB gun in that fashion was when one of my poorly aimed shots managed to somehow finally bring down a little bird. My excitement immediately turned to sorrow as I watched him fluttering helplessly to the ground. He was badly wounded but was not dead! What had I done? He had not harmed me, and it was too late to take back what I had done to him!

I cried as I watched him die. That was the end of my BB gun being used for anything other than trying to hit tin cans. It was just a lesson learned along the way that has stayed with me until this day.

93

Daddy sees the Death Angel

Daddy died on April 10th, 1987, at the age of 77. He was a Christian man who had lived his life, raised his family, stayed married to the same woman for 52 years, made his living and died in the town he loved best, and made his mark and legacy in ways that perhaps few knew about.

But I want to relate to you an experience shortly before his death. Dad had some health concerns in his later life, and he was a bit careless in managing them. Finally the ravages of diabetes overtook him, taking a toll on his eyesight and causing unsteadiness in his walking.

Daddy was in Waterman Memorial Hospital in downtown Eustis when my family and I came to town from North Carolina. We knew that he was very seriously ill and we spent a few days in town, visiting him often. And then the time had come for us to depart for our North Carolina home, and I was sitting by his bedside engaged in some conversation. Suddenly he looked past me. After a transfixed gaze lasting a few moments, he said "Isn't she beautiful!"

Fully expecting to find when I turned my head in the direction of his gaze, a lovely nurse or other attractive lass, I found instead a blank wall! No one was there at all! But I quickly answered his statement, "She sure is, Dad."

Had we known that his death was imminent we would not have left Eustis. As we drove up Orange Avenue and on out toward Cassia, I cried as I told wife Sylvia about Daddy's strange words. I told her that I knew I would never see Daddy alive again on this earth, and I thought that he had seen an angel in his room. And that God had allowed him a glimpse of an immortal being. She agreed with me.

Much quicker than we thought, the phone call came telling us of his death. Throughout the whole funeral and burial process it was comforting for me to know that Daddy, who always loved the beautiful things of life, slipped into eternity in the company of a beautiful angel. I think it was God's last earthly gift to Herbert John Greenlee as he brought him home.

94

Aunt Rose, Mama's Friend to the End

Probably the closest friend in Eustis that my mother ever had was Rose Wingfield. "Aunt Rose", as we kids called her, was a part of our lives from our earliest memories. Mama and Rose were part of the fabric of the First Baptist Church from the late 1930s through the mid-1980s.

We always looked forward to the ride out Washington Avenue extension to Ohio Boulevard where Aunt Rose lived. Her son Julian Jr. was a couple of years older than my siblings and me, and it seems that he always had some sort of gadgets to entertain us. One that I recall was a record machine; one that even in the late 1940s was an old one!

The records, instead of being round discs, were cylindrical, not unlike a toilet paper roll. He would slide them on an arm of that machine and put the needle down on it. Properly wound, it would then give us music!

But I mention Aunt Rose and Julian, because as the Lord works things out for us, in their later years Rose and Mom were able to continue their friendship in another state! After he was grown, Julian, his wife and family moved to the Raleigh, North Carolina area. And it was quite some years later that my family and I settled in Chapel Hill, just 30 miles from Julian. We just did not know it.

After many years working at the Ford dealership in Eustis, Julian Sr, died, and Aunt Rose went to live with her son in Raleigh. And sometime later, in 1987 after my Dad died, Mama came to live with my family. I cannot remember just how we discovered that Aunt Rose was so close by, but when we did, Mama and Rose were able to visit one another again as in the olden days. You should have heard the reminiscing going on!

Their close relationship continued until Rose died. It would be a few years later, in 2002, that Mama would join her best Eustis friend yet again, this time in heaven.

95

Refusing to Make an "Ass" of Myself

You probably couldn't get away with this today in our public schools, a play that refers to God and the Bible, but I participated in the Junior-Senior play in my junior year, 1954. Though I played the part of the prophet Isaiah in the play, I remember nothing about it, except that I was dressed in a robe of some sort. But one of the lines I had to say I have not forgotten!

I was the opening scene, coming out on the stage by myself with a spotlight on me. And there I would give a rather lengthy soliloquy from the scriptures.

It came from Isaiah chapter 1, and the line was in verse 3: "The ox knows his master, and the ass his master's crib, but Israel has not known me." I knew that I would have trouble saying the word "ass" in front of an audience. Heck, even though it was in the Bible and I knew it meant a donkey in there, the word was a naughty word in my house, referring strictly to a private part of my anatomy. So every time that I gave my little speech during rehearsal, I would break down in a fit of embarrassed giggles upon reaching the "ass" word. You know how it is. Once you get fixated on something that turns your tickle box over, it only gets worse!

I pleaded with Dorie Hostetler, the director: "Don't make me say that line. I'll mess up the whole speech!" She told me that it was a very important line in what I was saying, and it would stay in. Well, I fretted over that little 3-letter word until finally I decided to give the speech my way anyhow.

And folks, it went perfect! They say that I actually did a really good job out there! With all those eyes watching me from behind the side curtains, expecting me to mess up, I spoke with confidence. When I reached that line, I simply said "The ox knows his master, but Israel has not known me." No "ass" line! No giggles! And I maintained a very stern prophet-like voice throughout the speech!

I did not let a little 3-letter word make an "ass" outa me! (heh heh)… And from those earlier experiences on the stage, I found that I actually enjoyed taking part in plays, and have been in several in my adult life.

96

Christmas: A Time of Mixed Emotions

In the 1940s many of our Christmas holidays were spent at the home of our grandparents at Bartow. One Christmas Eve there came a knock on the door, and upon it's being opened, there stood Santa Claus! By George, he was believable! We kids had younger cousins with us at Gonga's that night. I am sure that they were enthralled by his appearance. But to my siblings and me, it was apparent that it was really Uncle "Red" all decked out like St. Nick. He made a good Santa, as his face was ruddy and quite round.

John, Miriam and I were never taught to believe that there was a real Santa Claus. That knowledge did not make Christmas any less meaningful, and I don't remember ever discussing "Santa belief" with the other kids of our childhood. But I must admit that Christmas was not one of my favorite holidays as I was growing up.

One of the many things that I dreaded about school in those early days was going back after Christmas holidays. Invariably the well-meaning teacher would ask each child to stand up and tell everyone what he and she received for Christmas. I learned through that experience that the practice drew a line between the "have's" and the "have not's" among the various families. It seems that it was my lot in life to have to follow some kid who received a new bicycle, or a fancy BB gun, or such.

Christmas shopping for us kids in those tough economic times for our family took place mainly at Kress's 5 & 10 Cent Store in Orlando. Daddy would give each of us a five dollar bill to buy presents for the other 4 family members. And of course we would each receive presents from our parents.

I remember that shopping as being some fun, because five dollars back then bought quite a bit more than it does today.

One of those purchases by me for my mother is still with us after 70 years or so as I write, at our home in North Carolina. It is a little deer standing on a glass body powder container, and it sits on the dresser in our guest bedroom.

The real joy in Christmas for me now is to see the happiness in the faces of other family members and friends as we gather to celebrate. And as we give thanks to God for the gift of His Son Jesus, whose birth we honor at that time.

189

97

Leaping into the Chicken Yard

I recall several acts of foolhardiness, or bravery as I thought them then. Just down Barnes Avenue from the house there was a stand of three very big oak trees! In the largest of the 3, we neighborhood boys had built a tree house on one of the lower limbs. The limb that held it was quite sturdy and we had lots of fun in that contraption.

But there were limbs above us – far above us – that were smaller in size, and at heights that would kill a kid if he fell. I remember shinnying up one of those limbs and actually walking out on a branch that bent under my weight, while steadying myself by holding on to an even smaller branch above me. Do you know that it did not even occur to me that a tumble from there would most likely be fatal! I was simply demonstrating my bravery to my buddies who waited their turn to do the same thing! Yeh, we all grew up.

Another that comes to mind is the leap from our garage roof into the chicken yard. As we boys stood looking up at the edge of that roof, it seemed alluringly close to the ground, close enough to jump from it into the chicken yard that abutted the garage. After some short discussion about what a great idea it was to leap from it, we took the old ladder from the garage and leaned it up there. Up we scrambled until the three of us stood close to the edge, peering down in the chicken yard, now several hundred feet away. Well, so it seemed. Actually it *was* 9 or 10 feet down there.

The place we had chosen as our landing area was a relatively clean part of the chicken yard (important) and the gray Florida dirt was soft in that spot. But you know, in spite of all the brave talk about this venture, I was actually terrified! I reckon it was here that I first realized that I had a problem with heights! Terrified but determined to follow through on this jump! No chicken me!

Finally, after a few "You go first!" "No, you go first!"s, one of us hurtled through space toward that tiny landing area! And after his safe arrival without injury, it became a little easier for the other two to make the leap! But I guarantee you that it was my first and last jump from that roof! Reckon that made the chickens happy!

Acrophobia remains with me to this day, but I think it was born on our garage roof over-looking the chicken yard on Barnes Avenue around the year 1950.

98

Successful Venture into Local Politics

I was a senior in high school when I was asked if I would run for student city councilman. Each year there was a day set aside for Eustis High School students to take the place of city officials. This meant that you got to ride in a car in the George Washington's Birthday parade.

Well, I was flattered that they asked me to run for something, but quickly dismissed the idea mainly because I would have to give a campaign speech in front of the students assembled in the auditorium! Even though I was taking a speech class, I was terrified at the thought of getting up there in front of those kids and teachers! After all, I was not Mr. Popularity in any sense of the word, and thought I would be dismissed with laughter at my even trying to run for the office.

The time for my speech was coming up in a few days, and I was pretty well told that I would be expected to participate and I might as well get used to the idea. Lord have mercy, what was I gunna do? I laboriously wrote down a few simple words about my qualifications for the position (hah!). Also I had taken about 10 little sheets of toilet paper and rolled them up. Maybe I could make a stab at some humor before I died out there!

On that fateful day, I sweated it out on the stage waiting for my turn to speak! You know, though, an auditorium full of young teens can be cruel, but they can also be an easy audience. As I stood up to speak I noticed that our school custodian, Mr. Allen Bunte, was sitting in the balcony, taking in all of the speeches. He became a part of my speech on the spur of the moment.

With all eyes on me, I began to speak in my most authoritative voice, "Teachers, Students, Ladies, Gentlemen ...and Mr. Bunte...in...the balcony to...my...<u>right</u>!" I then gave a forceful gesture in his direction. All eyes turned from me to Mr. Bunte just like that! He was roaring with laughter, and then so did the students! "Great start, James," I thought.

I followed that with something like "I have just a few words to bring to you this morning" and at that moment I let the rolled up toilet paper unroll clear to the floor! More laughter! Much calmer now, I still stammered through some mostly contrived qualities that I possessed and then sat down. Folks, to my absolute amazement I got a great round of applause from that group!

Well, the vote took place for the positions, and I was again stunned to find out that I had actually been voted in by a comfortable margin! I must say that it was at that point that I decided that being in front of a crowd was not the worst thing that could happen to me! Just keep 'em laughin'!

99

Soap Bubble Let-Down

I may have been thirteen. That's close to being right, so the year was probably 1950. To set the scene, the reader needs to know that there was a window right over our bathtub. Evidently the back porch had been an "add on" and now the window opened right in to it. Daddy had painted the window pane a pale green so that privacy in the bathroom could be enjoyed.

I was in the bathtub and Miriam and several of her friends were in the living room. As I was bathing, I noticed that a fairly thick layer of soap bubbles was forming on the water. My mind began to wonder if I could make enough bubbles to cover the entire surface of my bath water. And, shoot, the water was deep enough so that if I lay down flat in it, I would be completely submerged except for my head and toes. What if I were to try something a little risqué? Heh heh…

My adolescent brain thought it to be a good idea! So I worked for some time rubbing that bar of Lifebuoy until I had achieved my goal. I lay down and sure enough, the only parts of me showing above that thick layer of bubbles were my head and toes.

Next, I shoved up the window and yelled for Miriam and her friends to come to the porch! They did. By now I was lying flat discreetly covered by the layer of bubbles. I called them to the window and said, "Look at me!" Baaad mistake!

Three twelve-year-old girls were now peering intently into the tub where I lay grinning up at them! Their startled faces immediately gave way to shrieks of laughter! Folks, those soap bubbles that I had put so much faith in had let me down…in the worst possible spot!

It took me awhile to live that one down.

100

Reflections on My Great Sister

John and I had a very fine sister. Glenda Miriam Greenlee had a personality that made her popular among our friends and her school mates. I reckon she took more after our daddy in temperament, and her quick wit made life interesting for us.

And though I did not appreciate it as a brother who figured that being seen in public with a younger sister not a cool thing to do, Miriam was quite attractive. Someone sent me a picture of her recently. She was about 14. She was perky and opinionated, and was a very soft-hearted child and young woman who had a special love for cats.

Marrying very young, she left our home to begin a new life that people years older than her often have a hard time adjusting to.

She was a hard-working young lady who did her best to balance the rearing of two youngsters with her contribution to the income of her household. At an early age Miriam was stricken with kidney disease that finally led to several years of in-home dialysis. Finally, in her mid-thirties she received a kidney transplant.

Through all of the years of poor health she continued her employment at a shoe manufacturing company, her faithful participation in the worship of her God, and her responsibilities to her family. And amazing to me, who by now was her very proud brother, she did all of this with a wonderful sense of humor! In fact, her bright outlook on life often belied the facts of her illness.

After the transplant, her general health improved to the point that she was almost the same healthy Miriam we had known before. Sadly, her life was tragically ended at the young age of 38 in an automobile accident while on her way to her job in Iuka, Mississippi. I don't want to dwell on Miriam's death, but rather on her abbreviated but well-lived life. I want to pay tribute to her in noting that those in all walks of life with whom she interacted, were and are better for it.

Her greatest legacy is found in the lives of her two children who carry on to this day the finest characteristics of their mother. I am the very proud middle child brother of 2 great siblings!

101

Trespassers Caught

I told you in a previous article that a few of us junior high age boys used to sneak into the Eustis Baseball Park. The old wooden grandstand was a nifty place to play...and smoke those used cigarettes. That's right.

We knew that the caretaker rarely came to the park between games. This particular day was the last time we too came there between games. Racing that day through the stands and down the center steps, we came face to face with him! Yikes! He wasn't supposed to be there! And he was not amused to find us there!

He lined the 3 of us up and began to accuse us of vandalizing the grandstand. Shoot, he was even demanding that one or all of us step forward and admit our guilt! We protested truthfully that we had had nothing to do with several damaged areas.

So he then told us that we had broken the law by trespassing but that he would let it go if we promised to refrain from this behavior in the future. It scared the heck out of me and put an end to these clandestine visits and my easy access to pre-owned cigarettes. It also left me fearing that, since the caretaker knew my family well, he would tell Mama of those ballpark visits. But to his credit he never divulged this information to her, at least as far as I know.

102

Answered Prayer Indeed

I have spoken of my great grandfather in previous articles. William Arthur Greenlee became a permanent "winter visitor" in the very early 1940s, living continually with us in Belmont Heights.

During the early years on Barnes Avenue while Grandpa was still with us, 1943 to 1948, our family took occasional trips to New Smyrna Beach. They were day trips as we were fairly close to that beach. In fact, New Smyrna was the family choice of beaches, rather than Daytona which was a little closer, because of an alleged dangerous "under-tow" at that beach.

As Grandpa got older, he would not take the trip with us. And the folks would make sure that we left the beach in plenty of time to get home before it got dark, to tend to any needs that he had. I tell you this to introduce you to a "miracle from God" that happened late one afternoon at New Smyrna Beach.

Daddy would always nose the Model A Ford into the sand along beside the road that ran by the beach. This had never posed us a problem before. But on this occasion, after we were loaded in the old jitney and ready to head home, she could not get out of the sand! We were stuck! I remember Mama, John, Miriam and me pushing on the back as Daddy spun the wheels, but it just got buried deeper! Towels under the wheels, and rocking it backward and forward did no good!

The hour was getting late. And there was no help readily available for us. What about Grandpa? I know that I was the biggest worrier in the family, and I was near a panic! For as far as I could see, we had run out of options for getting that Model A Ford back on the road!

I came from a very strong Christian family, and we had always been taught to believe in the power of prayer! I like to think it was my idea, but in deference to another family member who might have suggested it, it was decided that we would have a prayer meeting about the situation. We all stood by the car as Daddy led us in prayer that the Lord would make it possible for us to get on the road and back to Grandpa.

An atheist would scoff and call it pure luck, but the Greenlee family knew better! Daddy got in that car, and drove it right out of that sand trap and on to the road! In no time we were chugging toward Eustis, arriving a little after dark.

And when we got home, we found Grandpa with a blood-soaked towel! He had cut himself shaving early in the day, and the bleeding would not stop! Let's just say that he was right glad to see his family pull in! In no time, Daddy and Mama had him patched up with no further complications!

It was "faith-builders" such as this one that saw the Greenlee family through some pretty rough times during those years. And that same God is still at work as I write this some 65 years later!

103

State Theatre Fun

Ah yes, who could forget the great times we had on Saturday evenings at the State Theatre on Bay Street? When the folks finally relented and allowed us to go to the "show", we were still limited as to the movies we could see. So mainly it was the Westerns, now called "oater's," that found us in the Saturday night crowd.

It was much fun to watch Roy Rogers, Gene Autry, Hopalong Cassidy, the Lone Ranger and those guys bring justice to the old West! But watching those shows was only part of the fun! How about watching an older couple (probably mid-40s in age) react to the happenings on the screen! Oh yeh! There they sat every Saturday night on the front row of the balcony.

Now, Folks, even at our young ages, we knew that the "good guys with the white hats" were going to eventually win the fights. This couple seemingly did not know that! They would shout happily when the right ones finally prevailed. They would stand up and wave their fists at the "evil-doers" and make derisive remarks toward them. They would groan and cover their eyes when things looked bad for the heroes. We had never seen such goings on from adults in movies, nor have I seen such to this day!

I recall going to a movie there one time with Phil, a very tall teenager. (A real Mutt and Jeff combination we were.) Though he was only one year older than me, and we both should have paid for adult tickets, I looked so much more like a child beside him that I was given a child's ticket. I paid for it, knowing that I should have corrected the mistake. Occasionally when that crosses my mind, I have the tiniest twinge of guilt pass hastily through my mind. So I probably still owe the State Theatre 30 cents or so.

104

Daddy's Tender Heart

I have written of my father on several occasions. Daddy reported for a review of his draft status each time he should have during World War II, and he was always classified as ineligible for service due having a wife and 3 small children to support, so we were told. He did serve his country as an air raid warden for our neighborhood in Belmont Heights. I fully believe, though, that had he been called to fight in the war, Herb Greenlee would never have been able to pull the trigger when the occasion called for it.

Two incidents come to mind when remembering what a soft heart Daddy had: The first one took place on the highway between Bartow and Mulberry, Florida, probably near 1930. Daddy was living in Mulberry and had begun to date my future mom Kathleen who lived in Bartow. He rode a motorcycle to her house. One day, when riding in the rain on that highway toward Bartow, he came upon a cow that had been hit by a car. He stopped and went to the mortally injured animal. Daddy's heart was so crushed as he witnessed this suffering, dying animal, that he sat down and put his arm around it. He stayed there like that, crying in the rain, until the cow died. I reckon he was a mess when he finally arrived for his date.

Another incident I may have mentioned before: They were laying a new concrete sidewalk in front of Daddy's shoe shop on Eustis Street. The work was finished for the day and Daddy and several other businessmen were taking a look at it. The concrete was firming but not dry yet. They observed an ant walking on it. One of the men took his finger and pushed that hapless bug under the surface of the cement. Though saying nothing at the time, Daddy was appalled at this senseless act of cruelty. And after the men dispersed, he went back and carefully searched out and dug the little critter up. He took it inside and washed it off; and then he released it. If ants talk to each other, that one entertained the ant hill big time that evening with his experience.

Later, when I was marrying Sylvia and still in the Air Force, he asked me if I planned to stay in the military with a family. I told him that I would be doing that. His only comment was that he did not think that the military would be a good life for my family. As the years passed, however, he appeared very happy I had made that life choice, and seemed very proud of his military son and family.

105

Daddy, the Great Cook

I tell my age for sure when I bring up things like this: I don't know if Oleo was new on the market when I was very young (early 1940s) living in Belmont Heights and later on Barnes Avenue, but I do remember it coming as a "do-it-yourself" product. The Oleo was white, and along with it came a little teeny packet of coloring. Daddy would dump the contents of that packet into a bowl of Oleo and work it in until it was thoroughly mixed and had the coloring of butter. Later it seems that the Oleo came in a squeezable plastic bag with the color packet attached on the inside. One would break the packet and squeeze the bag until it had that butter-like look. No doubt Oleo was cheaper than real butter. We used it before any health concerns were known to exist with the contents of the real stuff.

I've told you that Daddy was the better of the cooks between our parents. I think maybe it's because he liked to cook more than Mama. And he had been a cook in a restaurant in Winter Haven in their early married life. Occasionally he would prepare fried steak for us – a real treat – with all the trimmings; mashed potatoes, gravy, and the like. I remember him with a dinner plate in his hand, using the edge of it to tenderize the meat. He'd whack away on it for awhile and it seemed to do the trick. It would be a few years before I realized that meat tenderizer also came in a bottle or packet.

Another meal we enjoyed from his skillet was fried fish. It was mullet from Hoke Dollar's Fish Market on Eustis Street downtown (I don't think many folks have a taste for mullet, but Daddy cooked it up nice). Along with the fish we would have grits and little round and flat pieces of fried cornbread that Daddy cooked up.

And he could make the best pies! His chocolate and lemon meringue pies were tops, but he enjoyed making butterscotch pies most of all! He coulda sold 'em!

Since Daddy's church day was on Saturday, he would always have our Sunday dinner prepared when Mama, John, Miriam and I got home from church. I did not inherit Daddy's cooking skills, as my wife and children will tell you.

106

Bicycle Adventures

Today bicycle trips of 5 or 6 miles are commonplace. But early in my teen years, say 1950 or 1951, with a brand new Firestone bicycle, the streets of Eustis were the limits of my travels. I recall the time that a couple of us guys decided to ride all the way to Mount Dora! Mount Dora was another town! I was thrilled at the thought that I could transport myself to another town! Reckon it didn't take much to thrill me in those days!

The 10 mile roundtrip took us from our neighborhood surrounding Barnes Avenue and down South Grove Street to the Old Mount Dora Road. We passed through Belmont Heights where I had lived previously, and made our way beside Lake Gertrude and up the long hill to Donnelly Street, the main street in Mount Dora.

On Donnelly Street is Pine Forest Cemetery where one of our second grade classmates is buried. She had become sick and died at Waterman Memorial Hospital. Actually I had been a little sweet on her, as much as my shy personality would allow me to be. Connie was well-liked among us, and even though some years had passed, we would sometimes pull in to that cemetery and search for her gravestone. We finally located it.

We would go to the drug store in the middle of the town of Mount Dora and I would have a cherry smash at the soda fountain. Those trips became less frequent as the excitement of being that far from home began to wear off, and we found other ways to occupy our time.

It may have been the last bike trip that I took to Mount Dora, when we decided to take the highway back to Eustis. After you left the town, and just after you passed the Dixie Drive-In on Highway 19, you entered the longest curve in a road in the United States (this is true, at least it was back in those days). About half way into that curve I ran off the edge of the highway and got tossed into a thicket of sandspurs! Even though I was no stranger to sandspurs, this was a painful event for me!

As the other guys laughed, I carefully disengaged myself from those torture plants. While doing so, I found a very fine Phillips-head screwdriver lying right there just waiting for me to pick it up! So sporting some thorns that would accompany me and my new screwdriver, I made it on home.

That ended my bike travels outside of Eustis, until several years later when Bill Andrews and I took a 100 mile roundtrip to Daytona Beach!

107

The 3-Wheeled Bicycle Built for Two

Don't rightly remember whose idea it was. But in our young teen years we neighborhood boys made ourselves several 3-wheel "bicycles built for two." Here's how it was put together: We would take the front wheel off of one bike. Next, we would loosen the axle nuts on the rear wheel of the other bike. Then we would slide the fork of the first bike onto the axle of that back wheel. Tighten the nuts and voila! A bicycle built for two!

We had fun riding those contraptions all over Eustis! And parking them was a breeze! No need for a kick-stand! We would just turn the front one at an angle to the back one, and there it would stand!

But folks, it's a wonder we didn't break our necks with those things! As we would ride them over uneven terrain, the fork on the back bike would slowly work its way loose from the front bike. In your mind's eye you can see what might happen if that fork came completely and suddenly disengaged from the front bike, especially at any speed at all! The rider in the back would be in for a very sudden stop for his bike but probably not for him!

I was never involved in any accident with this "flaw" in our invention, but we made frequent stops to re-tighten this connection.

108

Mean Trick at Pumpkin Pond

Out Orange Avenue (Highway 19), several miles past where East County Road 44 intersects it (LaRoe Corner), a turn to the left will take you down Thrill Hill Road. A little way down that road, on the right side, you would find Pumpkin Pond in my teen years.

There was a little stream that fed the pond, and it had eroded the ground through the years and the terrain around it looked a very teeny weeny version of the Grand Canyon.

Pumpkin Pond was a very small and shallow body of water. In fact, most anywhere one might fall from his boat, he would be in waist-high water. The water was not clear, however, and an unsuspecting person might assume it to be deep.

Teen boys can be quite cruel to each other, even close friends. I cannot remember why we even put a boat into that dinky little pond now, but a few of us guys were having fun paddling around. One of our boat occupants, Buddy, could not swim! He was a fine athlete, but despite his prowess on the sports fields and in the gymnasium of Eustis High, he was terrified of the water!

We had come fairly close to land when one of the guys began to rock the boat! Others soon joined in. Buddy became quite disturbed by this action that was actually beginning to bring water over the side of the boat! As he yelled for us to stop, the water continued to make the boat ride lower, and more water poured in. Frankly I too was a bit worried that if the boat went down, it might be over a hole or deep area we did not know about.

As the boat reached its saturation point and began to slowly slip under the water, Buddy hollered, "Okay, I'll just drown!" And he leapt over the side. One of the guys jumped with him holding onto his belt just in case! They both landed flat-footed on the bottom of Pumpkin Pond with the water up to their waists! While the other guys were laughing and trying to drag the boat on in to shore, Buddy was furious and I was relieved that we didn't have to try to pull him out of the pond.

Don't know if Buddy ever learned to swim, but I do know that his anger was short-lived and we all remained close friends!

109

Roped Into Praying

Sister Miriam, a year and a half younger, was a favorite target of mine to tease. She had a very good sense of humor and could dish it back to me quite well! One thing that really sticks out in my mind is her putting me on the spot several times in our church youth group.

Some Baptist Training Union leaders, being able to empathize with those young teens in the group, would do all of the praying themselves. But we had a leader who thought that one of the young ones ought to lead the prayers. You know, it would be great training for them in future church involvements and all that. But nothing can scare the pants off of a shy youngster more than being asked to pray out loud in public! At least me! And Miriam knew that I was afraid and that was her trump card!

When the time for the closing prayer would begin to draw close, you could look around and see kids beginning to squirm and trying to hide behind the person in front of them. I was one of them, I guarantee you! But I think that Miriam was really hoping she would be called on to pray. And I recall the several times she was called upon.

"Miriam, would you please lead our closing prayer this evening?"

I would grimace with my eyes squinting shut as I awaited what was coming. I was thinking, *No! No! Miriam, I'll kill you!*

Sure enough: "No, ma'am, but Jamie will!"

JAMIE WILL! JAMIE WILL! She did it to me again! She's dead meat!
Somehow I felt the obligation upon me to pray then, and I didn't have the

nerve to pass it on to someone else. So I would begin to stammer out some sort of prayer, having no idea what I just said! Somehow I got through those prayers, but my sister was no friend of mine following those meetings. Further, her promises to not do that to me again were hollow indeed!

110

Toilet Tissue Cigarettes

Somehow we stumbled on to toilet tissue cigarettes in our early teens! Right! We discovered that if one would take two or three squares of toilet paper and carefully roll them, voila!, a poor imitation of a cigarette or cigar had been produced! Licking and pressing the edge of the last bit of paper to the roll kept it tight!

You could light that vile thing and blow out the flame. It would then smolder just like a cigarette. And you could draw the smoke into your mouth and blow it out coolly like the adults who smoked the real McCoy! Inhale it? Lord have mercy, you better not, unless you were ready for a real coughing fit!

When Mama found out we were smoking thusly, she had made her disapproval of this device known. We were forbidden to play like we were smoking! Now enter an unwitting relative who came to stay with us for awhile. Mama and Daddy both worked in Eustis (Greenlee's Shoe Shop and Ferran's Department Store respectively), and this dear one was unaware of our mandate to leave the toilet paper smokes alone!

We showed her how to roll the "cigarettes" and she watched us smoke them. She really saw no harm in our doing it, and not knowing we'd been told not to, she even rolled the cigarettes for us! This indiscretion on our part came to a screeching halt when she told Mama what fun we had had that afternoon!

111

My Haircut Embarrassment

Haircuts were not very expensive in my childhood and teen years. Seems like 50 or 75 cents got you a good one from Morgan's Barber Shop on Magnolia Avenue, or Acie's Barber Shop on Eustis Street. But looking for ways to save a little money, Daddy purchased a set of barber's hair clippers, and thus began our "homemade haircuts".

I don't remember brother John ever complaining about his haircut, and I did not ever tell Daddy of my disappointment in his clips, but they caused me some embarrassment at school. Knowing that I had a liking for a good flattop cut, he did his best to give me one. Basically, at least to me, it looked nothing like a flattop, but more nearly like a Mohawk! The sides would be cut very, very short, and on the crown of my head would be a rather narrow strip of hair, flattened on the top. I would think, *God, please let it grow back real fast!* But when it did grow back, it would be time again for another "Mohawk".

Once Daddy loaned those clippers to a neighborhood friend's father, who gave his boy a haircut. It looked so bad that the poor kid wore a stocking hat until it grew back in. His dad never tried it again.

As the years passed and Daddy's hair deserted him on top, he began to give himself haircuts. He simply buzzed the clippers over his head until all hair was gone! This he did until he died in 1987. Guess who inherited the clippers? Me! Guess whose hair has deserted him on top? Me! Guess who now buzzes his head with those very same clippers? Me!

112

Daddy and the Spook House

Halloween had to be Daddy's favorite holiday of them all! I have written of the funhouses and cookouts of my childhood during that celebration! There was another time that his abilities to entertain were put to good use.

Eustis High School had a big Halloween party one year, probably in the early 1950s. That shindig included a huge spook house set up in the back end of the building out across the softball field, called the Band House. Don't remember if Daddy was asked to help by the school, or whether he just volunteered his services. But the spook house was a great one!

In a particularly dark area of the winding path through it, he had utilized his Webster-Chicago Wire Recorder, by taking a short piece of the recording wire and recording in a desperate and wavering voice: "Hel-l-l-l-p…Let me out!" Somehow Dad had taken that little short wire and had it so that it continually looped through the head, so that a youngster arriving at that spot would hear the voice coming from some kind of a dark, cage-like apparatus, and being repeated over and over every five or six seconds. Daddy had it rigged so that something an approaching kid would step on would activate the switch to the recorder, and then turn it off as he left that part of the path.

It was a great Halloween party and the spook house was a big hit!

113

Mama Solves our Family Transportation Need

It must have been 1949 or 1950 when our family car, a 1929 Model A Ford, had just about reached the end of it's useful life, that Daddy had taken a trip to Indiana on the bus. Mama, who was working in downtown Eustis at that time, recognized the need for other transportation for the family. It seems to me that she was walking the mile and a half to her work.

One afternoon she came driving home in a very good looking light-green 1937 Chevrolet 2-door sedan! By jingoes, we had a "new" car! When Daddy got home he was elated that we now had a nicer automobile. He told Mama, "Somehow I just had a notion that you would have us another car when I got home."

Actually, even though it was at least 12 years old, it was in quite good mechanical condition and the inside was clean and well-upholstered! This young teen, who was "prouder" than he had a right to be, and had been embarrassed to be seen in the Ford, was very happy with the arrival of this vehicle.

That auto was the family car until 1952 when Mama's sister, Aunt Mary, bought herself a new Ford Mainline. She gave our family her old car, a black 1940 Ford. Seems we either gave the Chevy away or sold it at that time. I remember it having some suspension problems in the "knees" in the front end before it was no longer ours. I have mentioned before that the Model A was living its second life, without a body, in the early 50s, and the Greenlee boys were having a ball with it!

We did not have a lot by some standards, but we had love and the Lord, and that was more than sufficient!

114

Our "Dog Pan" Thermometer

Wintertime in Eustis! Though we had cold snaps during that season, it was more of an event for us to have actual freezing weather. Without a thermometer, we Greenlee kids had a foolproof way of checking to see if the ole' 32 degree mark had been reached.

In those early days of the mid-1940s, our front yard had a water spigot. And under that faucet the folks had placed a pan so that our dog, Little Brother, and other animals running loose in the neighborhood could have water.

On bitterly cold mornings, it was an exciting event for us to race out and check the dog pan to see if it was frozen over. For me it was very interesting that nature could actually make the water hard, something that we depended on the Crosley Shelvadore in the kitchen to do for us. Some of our neighborhood playmates had come from the north, and of course, nature-made ice was nothing new to them. Daddy was from Indiana and I suppose the thrill for him was more muted. But Mama and we kids were bona fide central Floridians.

I never saw snow in Eustis in my childhood; in fact, my first snow was experienced in Fort Worth, Texas in 1955 when I was 18 and in the Air Force.

115

Uncle Buddy's Scripture Quotes

I have mentioned before that my family often made the 90-mile trip from Eustis to Bartow, the town of my birth. One of the memories I have of our frequent visits to Gonga's house in Bartow was the whole family sitting around the large dining room table at mealtimes. Often there would be nine or ten of us.

One thing that was done at those gatherings was to have each person recite a Bible verse before Grandpa led us in a blessing for the food. I don't recall any of the verses that were used, except for two that my teenage uncle Buddy used, I reckon alternating them meal by meal.

They were two of the shortest verses in the Bible: "Jesus wept." (John 11:35) and "Rejoice in the Lord always, and again I say rejoice." (Philippians 4:4). Those verses tumbled out of Uncle Buddy's mouth something like this: "Je-swept" and "Rejoiceinalordalways, anaginIsayrejoice." Actually, the first verse became one word and the second one was two words the way he slurred them out.

Even at my young age, I always enjoyed hearing Uncle Buddy recite the scriptures at mealtime!

116

A Role Model for Sure

Allen Bunte (BUN-tee) was the custodian of Eustis High School during my junior and senior high school years of the early 1950s. Mr. Bunte was a friendly man whose other job was as pastor of the Cassia Baptist Church. I knew him quite well as he and Mrs. Bunte had previously been members of our church, First Baptist.

I can still see his long, lanky frame dressed in brown khaki shirt and pants and a happy smile on his face. It always seemed to me that he was a man at peace with things in his life, and he was a good example to us all. Mr. Bunte impressed me.

I know that I can easily get into trouble by singling out folks like I have just done. For there will be many fine people that I fail to recognize. But I will be bringing some of them to you as they come to my mind. We were blessed with so many role models in those days.

117

Regret

Do I have any regrets from my growing up years? Sure I do. Though life was basically all that I could have hoped for, I will mention an area that I would have tried harder to change if I could relive the grades 7 through 12 years. At least I hope so.

Scholastically, I would have wanted to be different! My elementary school grades were very good and I showed promise, I guess. But I frittered away my junior high and senior high school years, and in failing or barely passing the subjects, I lied, telling myself that any learning in those core subjects would be absolutely useless to me. But I knew better! The real truth behind my substandard performance after elementary school has to be labeled *total confusion*!

Gone were single classrooms with all subjects being taught by a single teacher each year. A six-year nightmare of subjects for me began, being taught by different teachers with differing personalities, in multiple classrooms. This brought about a precipitous decline in my grade point average and premature gray hair to my mom. It took two Summer School sessions and a long-suffering bandmaster named Bob Douthat listening to me blat away on the sousaphone for a semester, to give me a bare minimum number of credits to graduate.

In fact, it was still so close that on the afternoon of the 1955 graduation that would be that evening, I snuck into the school and went to the stage in the auditorium. The diplomas were up there just waiting. I also knew that any diploma that was not signed would belong to a person not graduating. I rifled through those diplomas until I found "James Greenlee" and with shaky hands opened it. IT WAS SIGNED! I had planned to skip the ceremony if I would not have been graduating with the class.

One of my teachers in my junior year became so frustrated with my poor performance that she went into my school records and retrieved my I.Q. score. She came storming back to class and called me to the front. Shoot, all in the class knew what my academic standing was, and I reckon they took her diatribe at me as a big joke. But she announced my score to them (couldn't do that today) and told me that she would never cut me any slack again. And she didn't.

In these modern times, after observing children who in many ways, student-wise, are the Jamie Greenlees of today with questionable behavior and study habits, I believe that I too had an Attention Deficit problem even as many of these are diagnosed now. Of course, in my school days, the only labels that seemed to fit were "bad boy" and "ne'er do well." I am making no excuses for myself and hold no ill will toward any, but I suppose I am trying to justify or at least understand in some small way my precipitous tumble to the near bottom of the class.

Why did I relate this unsettling time in my young life? Well, perchance a youngster might read this article, and he or she might realize that education opens the door to future careers and successes. If you need help, ask for it!

118

Callouses on My Fanny

In my days in the Eustis schools, disciplinary measures could be taken by school teachers, coaches and principals that today would lead to dismissals, criminal assault charges and lawsuits.

My folks had the philosophy that if I received corporal punishment at school, they would not put me in double jeopardy by re-punishing me at home. I really appreciated that!

My first paddling came in the fourth grade. The teacher had a system of allowing misbehaving pupils to control their own destiny. The first infraction put your name on the chalkboard. Each following instance of misbehavior would put a checkmark after it. Four checks brought a public paddling. You were brought in front of the class, made to bend over while the teacher whacked your fanny three or four times with a paddle style of her choice. I think her "seat warmer" looked sorta like a large ping pong paddle.

Starting in my junior high years, the frequency of my paddlings increased significantly. I may have been in the ninth grade when I peaked at 13 lickings in that school year! Right! I certainly wasn't the only kid receiving these, but I feel I may have gotten the most. (Could 13 in one year be a school record?)

I managed to spread my mischief throughout the classes enough that a number of my teachers, coaches and principals participated in my punishments.

I was a junior when I received my last paddling. It was administered by a coach who had lined a group of us boys up for some whacks for some school ground chicanery. I had not been involved, but was standing too close to those that were.

I have seen that coach many times through the years, and we are friends. I told him years later that I had not been involved on that occasion, and chided him for unjustly spanking me. He just laughed and said that that paddling made up for one I should have gotten but didn't.

Of course he was right.

119

Daddy's Physical Decline

Daddy was very proud that his health had always been good. He often boasted that he had never had a headache and had never taken an aspirin. In his later years, when he became diabetic, he refused to take the meds that could have prolonged his health for some years to come. And he continued to consume sugar-loaded food and drinks.

When Daddy told his doctor that he was not taking his medicine, the doctor said "Herb, I ought to take my belt off and beat hell out of you!"

Soon after, as Daddy continued to guzzle sugar-laden Cokes, Mom talked to his doctor about that. The doc said to just buy him what he wants. That would make him happy and life more peaceful. So the Cokes and other sugar sources continued to be consumed by Daddy.

A few years later, when Daddy was in Waterman Memorial Hospital sinking toward his death at age 77, he was sometimes out of his head. One day - and I am sure it was because he had an aversion to hospitals and medical treatments - he insisted that Mom drive him home in his hospital bed that he thought was his old car. Finally Mom had to make believe that she was trying to start that "car-bed". She made "starter noises" with her mouth and then told him it wouldn't start because of a low battery.

Brother John writes about the last time he and wife Ann saw Dad: "He was in Waterman and complained to me that his car was parked crooked (his bed was, I recall, at a 45 degree angle to the room). I told him that the car was OK, but that he was just sitting in it crooked. That satisfied him.

He also said before we left that he heard a cat purring. So I guess his last memories were of being in his car and hearing a cat purring - no better way for him to go."

It wouldn't be long until the Lord would take him to his permanent home.

120

Vocal Support for Mama's Candidate

It is November 2010 as I write this article. The mid-term elections have just taken place. We vote in my family and I am extremely interested in watching the returns come in! I remember the first time that I showed some passion for the election process.

Mama had selected a good man to support for the office of Governor of Florida, named Dan McCarty. Being quite the "mama's boy" in those days of the mid-1940s, I quickly picked up her enthusiasm for him too.

Probably a third-grader at the time, I commenced a very vocal campaign for Dan from our side yard! We had an old wooden swing back there, and I remember sitting in it and shouting over and over at full volume, "VOTE FOR DAN McCARTY!" Now, folks, I have never lacked for a voice that can be heard easily! I'm sure our neighbors could have stuffed a sock in my mouth!

Where along the way did I lose that type of passion for bold witness? Standing in the pulpit of my church each Sunday does not give me a pass on being bold in my witness for Jesus out among those of my community!

Oh yeh, as I recall, Mom's and my candidate Dan was defeated by a man by the name of (I think) Fuller Warren. But it durned sure was not my fault!

121

Major League Baseball Memories from the 40's and 50's

Ahh, the place of major league baseball in my life of the late 1940s and early 1950s! Several of my articles center on baseball. Maybe it was the "major" thing that brought excitement in my young life!

But to this day in the year 2010, I can recall the players and their positions on the Boston Red Sox team: Catcher- Birdie Tebbitts, 1st Base- Walt Dropo, 2nd Base - Bobby Doerr, 3rd Base - Vernon Stephens, Short Stop - Johnny Pesky, Left Field - Ted Williams, Center Field - Dom DiMaggio, Right Field - Al Zarilla. Star pitchers were Mel Parnell, Mickey McDermott, and Ellis Kinder. Billy Goodman was a great utility player.

New York Yankees starting pitchers were Allie Reynolds, Eddie Lopat, Vic Rashi, and Whitey Ford. Their big stars included Joltin' Joe DiMaggio, Yogi Berra, and Phil Rizzuto.

Cleveland Indians starting pitchers were Bob Lemon, Early Wynn, Mike Garcia, and Bob Feller. Stars were Al Rosen, Luke Easter, and Larry Doby.

The Brooklyn Dodgers, my close buddies Harold Webb and Alton Crawford's team, had star pitchers Preacher Roe, Don Newcombe, Carl Erskine, and Sandy Koufax. Great players were Roy Campanella, Billy Cox, Duke Snider, Carl Furillo, and Gil Hodges.

Some other players of note from my youth days are:

Ted Kluzewski - Reds

Ralph Kiner - Pirates

Ernie Banks - Cubs

Robin Roberts - Phillies

Willie Mays- Giants

Warren Spahn - Braves

Stan Musial, Bob Gibson - Cardinals

Lord, how I loved baseball in those days! Everybody needs a passion for something, and baseball sure was mine!

122

Daddy the Good Samaritan

In the days when our family car was a 1929 Model A Ford sedan, Daddy found out he could take the fan belt off and drive through fairly deep water without killing the engine. With the fan inoperable, it could not spray water on the spark plugs.

The intersection of Orange Avenue and Bay Street in Eustis was at a very low spot in the road. When heavy rain would come, that spot became a veritable swimming pool! Many a hapless motorist would attempt to drive through it and become stranded in the middle.

Often when things were slow in the shoe shop, Daddy would take the fan belt off of the old jitney and go push or pull these cars to higher ground. He never took any money offered for that service. He just liked to help.

123

Tree House Memories

Traveling south through central Florida down highway 95 at Christmas time 2010, I saw oak trees just like the ones that graced our Eustis yard on Barnes Avenue and in the neighborhood of my childhood and teen years in the 1940's thru the mid 1950's. No telling how many little boys and girls have played along Barnes Avenue in their shade since my days there. And surely some carefully inched their way out that sprawling limb to play on the platform tree house some 10 feet from the ground that Dale, David, John and I put up there about 60 years ago.

I think that the manufactured "tree houses" that grace the back yards of kids today, as nice and safe as they are, rob little guys of a sense of accomplishment and pride in building one from scratch.

124

Grandma Lake and Her Victrola

The Christmas trip to Gonga's house was an annual event during the 1940s. We three kids looked forward those days in Bartow with Mama's parents.

Grandpa's mother, Annie Mariah Anderson Lake, resided with them, and had her own suite of rooms down the right side of the house. Grandma Lake was not easy to get along with. She was very hard of hearing and was generally cranky. At least that's the way she presented herself to us kids. So even though we loved her, it was usually at a distance.

Grandma had a record player called a Victrola. You had to wind it up with a crank sticking out the side. I remember in one of her rare moments of civility to us, she invited us in to hear an old 78 rpm recording of the Christmas carol, "Hark, The Herald Angels Sing."

She put the record into the Victrola, and gave the handle one turn! After our childish suggestion that she might give the crank a few more turns, we were sternly advised that she knew how to use her machine and that our advice was not welcome!

So, John, Miriam and I were treated to the carol that went something like this: "Hark, the Herald... Angels....... siiing.......... Gllooooooorrrrry-y-y-y-y-y ....,,,," That was it! Our laughter was hard to stifle as we were ushered from her room!

125

Pianos and Our Love of Music

We inherited the old piano when grandmother Gonga died in Bartow. I remember it's being brought into the living room of our Barnes Avenue home.

I was so proud of myself when with my index finger I could pick out the tune to the Call to Worship "The Lord is in His Holy Temple" on that old piano. Sister Miriam took a few lessons and could play a little. Mama could play quite well.

We were a singing family. All 5 of us could carry a tune and participated in the music programs of our two churches. But my remembrance just now is the fun that Miriam and I had singing duets at that old piano. Actually we sounded pretty good if I must say so myself. One I recall was "I Was Lookin' Back to See."

After we grew up and went our various ways, wife Sylvia, and our two children would visit Miriam and her family in Mississippi, and again we would sing around her piano.

When Daddy died in 1987 and Mama became a member of our household in North Carolina, that old piano on Barnes Avenue was passed on to another grateful family. I hope that happy singing still takes place around it.

126

A Hard Lesson About Rudeness

Ahh, the joys and thrills of being able to operate a vehicle! The following incident takes place at the corner of Magnolia Avenue and Bay Street. Let's put the year at probably 1953. Our star today was old enough to have his license.

So Phil and my brother John were cruising Eustis in Phil's folks late model Packard car. It had an automatic transmission. Coming down Magnolia, Phil stopped okay at the traffic light that hung in the middle of the Magnolia/Bay intersection. Well, I say okay, but according to Brother John, he did stop with the nose of the car a little too far into the intersection. So, like any thoughtful driver would do, he put his car in reverse and backed up a few feet. (Maybe you can see this one coming…)

So now, Phil and John were waiting for the light to change. And behind them pulled up another vehicle. The trouble began and things went south as the light turned "green". The motorist behind was either in a very big hurry or else he was one of those impatient drivers that considers all other motorists to be a nuisance. He immediately lay on his horn! BEEEEEEEEP!! Ooooo…bad move!

This rude gesture from the car behind would be answered by Phil deciding quickly to floor his accelerator and lay rubber as John and he would speed away! (Bet you see it coming now… Remember that Phil had backed up earlier.)

The engine snarled and the car responded to Phil's foot on the accelerator! But guess which way it went: Right! Backward! The collision damaged both vehicles. Many years have passed, but I bet neither driver ever has forgotten that day! And I also would guess that the impatient driver is a bit more cautious in his horn-blowing.

127

Harrowing Boating Adventure

This event took place in the late 1940s. What a great idea! Although our family was not involved in "boating" in any way, Daddy thought it would be fun for us to "go fishing in a boat!" In my early years we had lived on West Crooked Lake in Belmont Heights, just outside of Eustis on the Old Mount Dora Road. And we did like to fish the "old fashioned way," standing on the bank and wetting our worms on the end of cane poles. But, hey, fishing from a boat might be fun indeed!

So, Daddy took us to Lake Yale, near Eustis and off the road to Grand Island, to a place where one could rent a boat and a little outboard motor. Knowing not a lot about boats, motors and proper water precautions, we were off! Mama, Daddy, John, Miriam and me. Although I have never been a "fan" of deep water, it did seem like fun as we chugged along!

Never mind those little poles sticking out of the water, put there (we were later to learn) to warn boaters to stay away from underwater hazards in certain areas. Our old wooden boat plowed straight ahead, right into one of those "danger zones."

Suddenly, and without warning, we came to a screeching halt!! Our boat was now perched precariously upon an underwater piling, still remaining from a long ago dock that had been located there! The floor of the old wooden boat was raised up in the spot where the piling was, and in the opinion of this little boy, we were in danger of sinking if it broke through! I think Daddy and the rest of the family thought the same thing.

Praise the Lord, we were still near enough to the boat rental place for them to hear our yells for help! And quickly another boat was alongside us, to pull us safely off of the piling and back into safe water! After Daddy received some kindly instruction from the occupant of the rescue boat, we went on to enjoy the day. But this event made a lasting impression on a little boy who was already a bit wary of being in water over his head!

128

Fresh Cement Temptation

In a nearby neighborhood in North Carolina where my wife and I often walk, there is a sidewalk that contains a freshly poured concrete square. Each time we pass over that square my mind goes back to probably 1948 or so. Because etched permanently in that otherwise smooth surface are 3 letters, obviously the initials of some lad or lassie.

Three friends were making their carefree way up Grove Street from Barnes Avenue on the way to spend a few coins at Hunsucker's Service Station on the corner of Palm Avenue and Grove. About halfway on the large city block between Lakeview and E. Doane Avenues and near a giant oak tree, Jim, Raymond and Jamie (that's me) came across a freshly poured concrete square in the sidewalk. I mean it was so fresh it was literally shouting at us to make our marks on it! There was even a stick nearby! Honest, folks, I was not the culprit this time even though I could have been. The process of elimination says it was Raymond using the stick. I'll explain.

In letters about six inches tall, Raymond began to write "J...I..." Jim then realized that Raymond was not writing his own name! Jim's name was the only one that started with those letters, and he objected loudly! "Don't you dare put _my_ name on that!" So Raymond finished the letters with his first one, "R". Yep, it read J I R. For many years that block was there, and there are only 3 lads who knew what those initials stood for. Checking recently (year 2015) I am sad to report that this square of sidewalk no longer exists.

129

Mama's Cedar Chest

When times were bad economically for our family in the 1940s, Daddy would try to supplement his income in various ways. He sharpened lawnmowers at home, the old push kind. I remember him also sharpening a few power mowers. Another venture was his putting cedar chests together from kits, and then adding the finishing touches. And I must say that he did a splendid job on them. These he sold for a modest profit.

For Mama's birthday one year in the late 40s, Daddy made her a large cedar chest. It was beautiful and he had put a decorative picture of a ship at sea under full sail, on the front of it. That chest sat proudly in the corner of their bedroom in our house on Barnes Avenue, and Mama stored her most prized possessions and keepsakes in it. Things found in there meant that they were very important to her. After Daddy died in 1987, that cedar chest and Mama came to live with us for the remaining 15 years of her life.

As I write this in the year 2012, some 65 or so years after Mama received it, that old cedar chest graces the guest bedroom at our home in North

Carolina. The finish is now less than perfect, and the ship in the picture on the front is hard to make out. But the chest itself is strong and still contains a lot of those things that Mama cherished.

130

Epilogue

This article brings down the curtain on my "growing up in Eustis" years. And it opens the door to the next 21-year segment of my life. It involves leaving home but taking with me three friends from my childhood and teen years. Four of us guys went over to Leesburg and made arrangements to join the Air Force. Three of us were too young to do it on our own, and we each had to get parental consent. As I write, there are two of the four of us remaining and we might differ somewhat in our remembrances about just how those "joining up" events unfolded. So I will tell it my way.

High School graduation day in May of 1955 had come and gone. And the ensuing summer was fast turning into fall. To be honest I was a 17 year old young man without a plan whatsoever about what to do with the rest of my life. Some of my friends were heading off to college at the University of Florida or Florida State University, Stetson University or other institutions around. My grades kept me from even the thought of doing that. That was perhaps my first inkling that all the fooling around that I had done in high school might not have been such a good idea after all.

I had been working for a while on Saturday's at the local Winn-Lovett (later Winn-Dixie) grocery store on North Eustis Street as a bagboy. This brought me around $7 plus tips for that day's work. One day in late August, word came to me that friends Dick Floyd and Bill Andrews were going to the Leesburg Post Office to talk to the Air Force recruiter. The Air Force? I had always assumed that I might someday end up in the Navy, but how about the Air Force?

I decided along with my buddy Alton Crawford to go along to watch the proceedings on that fateful day in Leesburg. Alton and I sat at a picnic table outside the post office, next to the one with the recruiter and our two friends. As the recruiter gave his spiel about the glories of a military enlistment and maybe even a career, our interest became quite intense. Hey, 30 days paid vacation a year, $78 a month to start out. Alton and I soon moved over to the table with them.

So okay, we four boys thought it would be a good idea to join the Air Force. But as I said, 3 of us needed to get our moms and dads to sign off on it. I personally think that though Mama and I had a very close relationship, she thought it would be good for me and help me to grow up and get started in life. Daddy was a very sentimental man and I think it hit him pretty hard to think that his second born would now be leaving the nest. John had been off to Florida State University the previous year, and Miriam was married and living elsewhere. But with the folks' signatures on the appointed lines, I along with the other three made my way to Leesburg on August 31st, 1955, to catch the Greyhound Bus bound for Jacksonville.

As I sat on that bus looking out at Mama and Daddy waving to me, I knew that I was saying goodbye forever to my familiar and comfortable way of life, and stepping through the door to a future about which I had no clue. I quietly shed some tears but I knew that I was not the only one on that bus doing so.

Since that day in August of 1955, I have never lived in Eustis again. But my ties through family and friends have remained strong there through the years, and to this day I still go back to visit once in a while. And I shall often return in memory to the dusty clay roads of my childhood as long as I live.

Jamie

Printed in the United States
By Bookmasters